PERFECT MIND:
PERFECT RIDE

Sport Psychology for Successful Riding

PERFECT MIND: PERFECT RIDE

Sport Psychology for Successful Riding

INGA WOLFRAMM

Foreword by Mary King MBE

KENILWORTH PRESS

Copyright © 2015 Inga Wolframm

This edition first published in the UK in 2015
by Kenilworth Press, an imprint of Quiller Publishing Ltd

Reprinted 2017, 2019

British Library Cataloguing-in-Publication Data
A catalogue record for this book is available from the British Library

ISBN 978 1 910016 04 6

Designed by Arabella Ainslie
Jacket photographs by Nikki De Kerf

Printed in Malta

Kenilworth Press
An imprint of Quiller Publishing Ltd
Wykey House, Wykey, Shrewsbury SY4 1JA
Tel: 01939 261616
E-mail: info@quillerbooks.com
Website: www.kenilworthpress.co.uk

CONTENTS

There is freedom waiting for you,
On the breezes of the sky,
And you ask "What if I fall?"
Oh but my darling,
What if you fly?

by Erin Hanson

FOREWORD

How do you become a successful rider? I've been asked this question many times and it's never easy to come up with an answer. The rider, the horse, the training, the facilities, the support team – eventually all these elements need to come together to form a whole.

And yet, I'm convinced that it all starts with the rider. First and foremost, riders must want to be around horses and do their best for them. If they want to go all the way, riders have to live and breathe the sport. Looking back at my own life as a rider, I've been passionate about horses for as long as I can remember and I never wanted to do anything else. Working with young horses, bringing them on, step by step, and developing their talents so that one day, maybe, I'm able to compete with them at the highest level, that's a real privilege and one I wouldn't give up for the world. What is more, I believe that if my horses are happy, if they enjoy their work, trust in me as their rider and have been brought on to cope with what's ahead, they'll end up showing their true potential.

As a result, I believe that, as riders, we'll need to work on ourselves, every second of every day. Being patient and remaining calm and quiet at all times, regardless of whether we're going for a hack around the block or are about to perform at a major competition, whether we're at the top of our game or things aren't working out quite the way we'd hoped. Anyone who wants to get to the top of their chosen discipline will have to deal with the inevitable highs and lows. They are all part of the experience: one day you'll win an event and the next you'll hit the deck.

In my mind, in order to cope with the uncertainties, the ups and downs, with the successes and failures, with winning and losing, you first of all should know what you want. You should have a dream and be single-minded about achieving it. When I look back at my own career, I can honestly say that I've always been exceedingly determined. I don't think I would have got to this level if I didn't have this drive to win. But I am also very calm and very level headed with an even temperament. There's no point in getting cross or upset when things go wrong; you're going to have to, quite literally, ride out whatever is thrown in your path.

In my view, those are also key skills when it comes to dealing with the pressure of competing. Lots of riders feel nervous before an important event, but it's how you deal with those pre-competitive flutters that is going to make the difference. In order to be able to do what you have to do you'll have to learn to control that anxiety. You'll need to develop a system that works for you. To me, being very organised helps. On the morning of a cross-country day, I want to be sure that I've got everything in place, that I've got my clothes, my stop watch, everything in piles, so I know that there's no panic at the last minute. Then I like to do the last course walk on my own, making up my mind how I am going to ride it. I always keep my thoughts positive, and see myself doing well in my mind's eye.

But even if things end up going wrong or you've made a mistake, don't get hung up about it. Once again, it's part and parcel of the sport. It is how you deal with these situations that is going to determine whether you'll end up doing well or whether you'll fall to pieces. It's essential not to dwell on what has happened. Instead, act on the reason why the mistake happened, focus on what's ahead and carry on positively.

It all comes down to this: as riders, we need to be in control of ourselves, of our thoughts and emotions, at all times. We need to be in control of our minds. Only then can we be in control of our bodies too, and ride our horses in the way they deserve to be ridden.

This book will help you to achieve just that. It'll teach you the mental attitudes and skills you need to become the very best you can be. It'll help you achieve the 'perfect mind' for a 'perfect ride'.

Mary King, Olympic three-day eventer

PART I

ATTITUDES THAT KEEP YOU GOING

INTRODUCTION

WHY SPORT PSYCHOLOGY MATTERS

It's the year 1991, a few days after the four-star eventing competition at Burghley, UK. A 23-year old Pippa Nolan eagerly rifles through the pages of the British magazine *Horse & Hound*. For the first time she'd competed two horses at that level and she's hoping for glowing reviews of her fourth and fourteenth place. Imagine her disappointment when she's greeted by the following comment by Captain Mark Phillips, former Olympian and eventing aficionado:

> '...two young ladies (referring to Pippa Nolan and Lucinda Murray) who won't be reliable at top level until they go back to basics and learn to ride across country properly.' [1]

What a blow to a young rider's confidence.

Fast forward to 2003, and Pippa Nolan, now Pippa Funnell, becomes the first – and only rider to date! – to win the Rolex Grand Slam; a feat that involves winning not one, but the three consecutive four-star events: Kentucky, Badminton and Burghley. Since that fateful comment twelve years ago, Pippa Funnell has turned herself into one of the best eventing riders in the world.

How did she do it? At the heart of her success lies a combination of talent, incredibly hard work, commitment to the sport, believing in herself, perseverance in the face of failure and coping under pressure. In a word, Pippa Funnell became mentally tough. She learned how to use mental skills to tremendous effect.

---

1   Funnell, P. (2004), *The Autobiography*, London, Orion Books

As a result, Pippa Funnell has been one of the most vocal riders about the value of sport psychology throughout much of her career, crediting much of her success to the honing of her mental skills. In her autobiography, she sums up the problem – as well as the solution.

> *'One of the conditions for receiving Lottery money is that riders are expected to take advice from specially appointed people like nutritionists, physiotherapists – and sport psychologists. (…) Sport psychology was pretty new then (ed: 1998) and most riders felt it was completely unnecessary; in fact all my friends thought it was hideously embarrassing and gave it a wide berth. But I wasn't embarrassed; I just pricked up my ears. I have always been open-minded to suggestions because I feel that if anything, however minute, can help me, it's a bonus.'* [2]

And what a bonus it turned out to be.

Over the past few decades researchers have shown in literally hundreds of studies that (sport) psychological concepts such as self-confidence, the ability to perform under pressure, handle setbacks effectively, commitment and perseverance are important contributors to competitive performance. Those performers (riders), who are able to hold it together mentally when the pressure is on almost always end up on top. What is more – and despite what many riders still think – the level someone rides at doesn't even come into it.

Surprised? Don't be.

You see, it's like this: regardless of whether you're just starting out or are a seasoned professional, the idea of proving your worth in front of any kind of audience, at an event, a show, or even at home, can be nerve-wracking.

The reasons are straightforward enough. In competition, you and a bunch of other riders are thrown into the ring together and expected to battle it out to see who comes out on top. But even if you're 'only'

---

2   Funnell, P. (2004), *The Autobiography*, London, Orion Books

riding at home, the moment someone decides to stand next to the arena to watch, they're highly likely to have an opinion of how you're doing. And then there's you. You've invested so much time, effort and money into the sport. You've sacrificed other areas of your life, be that school, friends, recreational activities or even a steady relationship for the sake of that one, all-consuming love. Your horses and your sport. Now you want to prove it hasn't been for nothing. Never mind how much pleasure you derive from being with your horse, from training and riding every day, deep down, you still want other people to approve of what you're doing. You want external validation – and a sure-fire way to get it is to do well in competition (or to have lots of people telling you that you're amazing).

And yet… competing (or strutting your stuff in front of an audience) can also be fun. In fact, it can be so exhilarating, that it becomes (almost) addictive. That feeling of you and your horse giving it your all, stretching yourself further than you ever have before, working as a team, a unit, as one. When it all comes together, it's incredible.

If it all comes together.

This is where sport psychology can make a real difference. Suddenly, training the mind becomes as important as training your horse, no matter whether you're a beginner or one of the world's best.

Making sure everything *does* come together depends in no small part on whether you, as a rider, are tough enough. *Mentally tough enough.*

Several groups of researchers, among them Professor Graham Jones, founding member of British consultancy firm Lane4, have tried to define this concept called mental toughness. In their eyes it's a psychological edge, that is either inborn or developed over time and that enables athletes to cope better than others with the stresses of sporting life: poor or outstanding performance in competition, being put under pressure by peers, trainers, the press, injury, setbacks in training, an isolating lifestyle. Due to their ability to cope, mentally tough athletes are generally more consistent than others when it comes to motivation, determination, confidence and keeping control under pressure.[3]

---

3   Jones, G., Hanton, S. and Connaughton, D. (2007), 'A Framework of Mental Toughness in the World's Best Performers', *The Sport Psychologist*, pp. 21, 243-264

In essence, what Jones and his colleagues are saying is that individuals who embrace the stressors of competitive sports end up outperforming their peers – not because they're necessarily more skilled or talented, but because they thrive on the demands of competitive life.

By now, top riders around the world are beginning to realise the importance of developing the right kind of attitudes and mental skills – and grassroots or amateur riders might wish to heed their words.

US dressage rider Catherine Haddad, who has numerous national and international Grand Prix wins to her name, firmly believes that training your mind is essential in any campaign to become a top class rider:

'You are not going to get anywhere without relevant mental skills. Really, you're talking about different kinds of skills (…) But the ability to maintain a positive attitude and to brush off setbacks and to remain tenacious that is something you need over the long run. That is something you need every day.' [4]

Let's be honest. Phrases such as 'maintaining a positive attitude', 'brushing off setbacks' and 'remaining tenacious' sound much more convincing coming from a top class rider than if delivered in a scientific paper. Partly, that's because it comes from real-life experience. And partly, it's because we admire those who've risen to the top of the equestrian tree – and wouldn't mind emulating them…

But just in case you're not convinced, listen to the words of dressage rider Wayne Channon. He represented Britain in both the 2005 European Championships and 2006 World Equestrian Games, and is convinced that the mind really matters:

'Everybody I know in the top of the sport, when they get on their horse, they are totally focused. They prepare themselves, and they work really hard at concentrating on what they are doing. This is crucial; you can't do it without that. If riders don't have the

---

4   Wolframm, I. (2012), 'Mind over Matter: How mental training can raise your game', *Horse Sport International*, Issue 2

necessary mental skills, they need to get them, as without them they can't go to the top.' [5]

If you still don't believe it, this is what one of the world's most accomplished Dutch dressage riders, Adelinde Cornelissen, thinks:

'Talent is not where you're going to make the difference in competition anymore. If you want to win, you need to have the full package. You need to be mentally and physically at the top. That's where all the little percentages can be gained in competition.' [6]

Surely that should do it!

The message couldn't be clearer: acquiring the right type of mental skills is an important step on the road towards optimal performance.

In order to be the best you can be, it's not enough to ride well. It's also not enough to work incredibly hard. In order to excel as a rider, you're going to have to be able to control your mind, and your body, your thoughts and your emotions, wherever you are and in whatever situation. What is more, you must learn to like, or even love, the pressure that goes hand in hand with competition and the all-consuming lifestyle of owning horses. At the same time, as you embrace stress and learn to reinterpret it as something positive, you'll also need to come up with your own definition of success, otherwise you'll run yourself into the ground. Then you'll have to try and cope with all the obstacles life as a rider throws at you and in your way. Luckily, there'll be those to help and support you – but you've got to find them first. Most importantly, you'll need to figure out who you want to be. Every day, you'll have to believe that you'll get there one day.

Sounds difficult? Yes, it does.

And yet, there are riders out there who are doing it. Meaning it is possible.

5   Wolframm, I. (2012), 'Mind over Matter: How mental training can raise your game', *Horse Sport International*, Issue 2

6   Ashton, R. (2014), Adelinde Cornelissen, this quote is from an article that first appeared in the May 2014 issue of *Dressage Today* magazine (DressageToday.com)

Right? Right! Take heart, then, and read on.

Developing the right kind of mental attitude, skills and routines that'll help you achieve optimal mental control isn't magic. These attributes can be learned, just like the technical skills of riding a horse.

That's what the following pages aim to do: teach you how to be mentally tough. How to be in control.

You'll learn how to define success for yourself, so that the ever increasing pressure from those around you doesn't hold as much sway anymore – or how to cope with the inevitable ups and downs of a (competitive) lifestyle with horses; how to believe in who you are and how to stay committed to your own journey towards success – or how to avoid self-sabotaging yourself just when things start to go well. Then there are the practical elements of mapping out your journey using the most effective goal-setting techniques. You'll be shown how to keep cool under pressure, how to reframe your thoughts to put you in an optimum frame of mind, how to keep focusing on the things that matter most, how to use visualisation to best effect and how to develop the kind of mental routines that give you confidence. Lastly, you'll be given tips on how to optimise your mental preparation on the weeks and days leading up to a show, how to make the most of the day itself, and how to evaluate things effectively once it's all over.

Most importantly though, adopting the right kind of attitude and developing effective mental skills will allow you to grow as a rider, improve the relationship with your horse and maximise your own performance in (and out of) the saddle.

Put simply, this book helps you achieve the *perfect mind* for a *perfect ride*.

CHAPTER 1

KNOW WHO YOU ARE – AND BELIEVE IN IT

'I set myself three goals in dressage when I was 20. I wanted to ride on the team with Carl; I wanted to ride at Olympia Horse Show – I'd sat in the grandstands as a teenager thinking this is the best place in the world to ride; and I wanted to compete in the Olympics.' [7]

Charlotte Dujardin

Then, it was a childhood dream. Now, it has become reality. Charlotte Dujardin, Olympic Champion, World Champion, European Champion, World Number One, World Cup Champion, record holder in the Grand Prix, the Grand Prix Special and the Freestyle – there's hardly a competitive title in the sport of dressage that this young lady hasn't won. And she managed to achieve it all on top of the 'other' wonder horse, the dark brown Dutch warmblood gelding Valegro, jointly owned by her mentor Carl Hester and Roly Luard.

While the story of Charlotte and Valegro is, of course, the most exceptional of fairy tales that will fuel the dreams of thousands of pony-mad girls all over the world, many top riders have a similar story to tell. Most – if not all – of them talk of one fateful horse, that either propelled them into the ranks of equestrian legends or even granted them lifetime membership. Think of John Whitaker and Milton, of Anky van Grunsven and Salinero, think of Ludger Beerbaum and Ratina Z, or Isabell Werth and Gigolo, think of Meredith Michaels-Beerbaum and Shutterfly or

---

7   White, J. (14th May 2014), 'Charlotte Dujardin, the girl on the dancing horse, determined to stay No 1', *The Daily Telegraph*. html: http://www.telegraph.co.uk/sport/olympics/equestrianism /10831210/Charlotte-Dujardin-the-girl-on-the-dancing-horse-determined-to-stay-No-1.html

Sir Mark Todd and Charisma, think of Pippa Funnell and Supreme Rock, or Mary King and King William. And, lest we forget, think of Edward Gal and the original black wonder horse Totilas…

Especially these days, the breakthrough at the very top simply isn't possible without a talented horse. After all, by its very definition equestrian sport depends on the four-legged athlete as much as the two-legged one (as well as on quite a few other things, some of which we'll be discussing in the course of this book).

But the question is, did Charlotte know she'd be an Olympic Champion when she first sat on Valegro? Did Anky have an inkling of the successes she'd achieve with Salinero? Was Pippa Funnell able to predict she'd win the Rolex Grand Slam on the back of Primrose Pride and Supreme Rock? Did John Whitaker know Milton would be the first horse to win more than £1 million in prize money? Did Edward Gal think he'd change the landscape of competitive dressage forever when he first laid eyes on Totilas?

No. Of course they didn't.

But they would have felt the potential. Then, they would have dared to dream.

At some point those dreams would have turned into something more specific. They would have become definite goals. Then, those riders, unknown and (relatively) unaccomplished at the time, would have chipped away at their dreams, step by step, achievement by achievement, until, one day, the opportunity of a lifetime presented itself.

Just like it did for Charlotte.

It started with her being asked to work for Carl Hester. She came to his yard for a lesson in 2007. In his autobiography Carl talks about suggesting to Charlotte that she might like to stay on for ten days to fill in for one of his staff, who was on holiday.

Of course she stayed.

After the ten days were over, Carl offered her a more permanent position, complementing the team of riders already working at the yard[8] –

---

8   Hester, C. (2014), *Making it Happen*, London, Orion Books

an opportunity no ambitious young rider would have passed up.

At some point, Carl decided to put his charge on the five-year old Valegro. And what a decision it turned out to be! The pair went on to win almost every British national championship, from novice onward.

After that, the rest, as they say, is history…

There are many more stories very similar to the one of Charlotte and Valegro. Stories of talented riders being given that special horse, the one of a lifetime. Stories of riders being allowed to hold on to their dreams and turn them into reality. Stories of riders 'making it happen' – which is precisely what Carl Hester said to his pupil just before she was about to enter the ring for her first Grand Prix at the 2012 Olympic Games:

'Don't forget, some people want it to happen, some wish it would happen, go and make it happen.' [9]

Which is exactly what Charlotte Dujardin did.

Unfortunately though, these modern fairy tales are all too frequently referred to as 'lucky breaks', as if the rider had done nothing more than being in the right place at the right time. A fallacy if ever there was one.

None of these so-called overnight success stories actually occurred overnight. None of the world's top riders 'suddenly' rose to the top. Every single one of them spent year after dedicated year honing their skill, knowledge and expertise in order to become the best possible riders and the best possible horsemen or -women.

According to Dr K. Anders Ericsson, Professor of Psychology at Florida State University, people have to amass approximately 10,000 hours of deliberate practice prior to joining the ranks of experts. While these are mere averages – and there are undoubtedly exceptions to this – Ericsson's rule translates to almost three hours of high quality, structured practice every single day for ten years. If you manage an hour and a half a day, it'll take you twenty years. If you only do an hour, it'll take thirty.

It makes you think, doesn't it?

---

9   Carl's words are actually slightly adapted from Michael Jordan's original 'Some people want it to happen, some wish it would happen, and others make it happen.'

Thirty years before you can call yourself an expert. And that's only if you're completely focused on what you want to achieve when you sit on your horse.

Every. Single. Day.

No ambling along on a long rein, checking messages on your phone. No idle chit chat with the person riding next to you. No deciding to take the day off because you've got other things to do…

In short, you need an incredible amount of dedication and commitment to amass the necessary hours to become an 'overnight success'.

What is more, every single top rider will have gone through the ups and downs that are part and parcel of a life with horses. Horses will, as well we all know, insist on being horses! All the detailed planning in the world amounts to nothing if a horse pulls a tendon, runs into barbed-wire fencing or gets cast in the stable. Coping with adversity is, unfortunately, an important prerequisite of getting to the top. We'll discuss this in more detail a little later on. Just for now though, suffice it to say that learning how to deal with the stresses of daily life teaches invaluable lessons on how to cope with the strains of performing whenever it matters most.

And yet – such 'coping skills' are merely one part of the equation. Yes, they do help you get through a situation and keep your head above the proverbial water. However, they do not stretch to making sure you stay true to yourself and your dreams despite or even because of all the struggles you've had to go through. Most importantly, they don't provide enough protection, enough of a buffer, for when you decide to venture forward into the unknown, putting yourself out there time and again on your quest to become something you really, really want to be.

So what, I hear you ask, does?

According to modern dressage legend Kyra Kyrklund it is all about believing in yourself. The Finnish rider is no stranger to how tough it can be to reach the top. Born in the Finnish capital Helsinki, Kyra was brought up in an entirely non-horsey family. Still, every year, the family would spend their summer holidays in a country cottage. Under the watchful eye of a friend of the family, a large animal vet, young Kyra soon learned all about cows, sheep, pigs and… exactly, horses. Whenever she didn't spend time with the vet, she could be found at the small farm run by her godmother.

This godmother also happened to have several coldbloods.

One fateful morning Kyra and one of the sons of her godmother decided to take a young mare out for a ride. Thinking back to that day, Kyra still shakes her head in disbelief. The mare was barely four years old. At one point, the young animal spooked and bolted. Both children lost their balance and toppled off her back. Not a big problem, one might think. After all, children regularly fall off their horses and ponies. But on this occasion Kyra's foot had got caught in the reins, and she was dragged along, behind the galloping horse, until, finally, a nearby farmer managed to catch the frantic animal. Despite the inevitable broken arm, Kyra was not to be deterred. She wanted to ride again. Her parents relented and soon after she was allowed to take her first real lesson at a riding school in Helsinki. To her great horror, the horse waiting for her looked just like that run-away mare from her godmother's yard. Kyra admits that, to this day, she's never been so scared.

'But even then I knew that I had to go through with it.' [10]

And that's precisely what she did. She wasn't to be deterred, no matter how scared she was, quire simply because she knew she wanted to ride. Nothing else would do. It was precisely that deep seated knowledge and determination, which would stand her in good stead a few years later when her international equestrian career started in earnest. Throughout the 1970s and '80s Finland couldn't offer an aspiring rider much in the way of support or training. Once again Kyra wasn't put off. She simply kept going until, finally, she managed to make her mark at the 1988 Olympic Games in Seoul. Her secret?

'Never, ever give up! Stay positive and keep working away at whatever it is you believe in.' [11]

---

10   Wolframm, I. (2012), *Dreamteam Pferd und Reiter: Persönlichkeitsbestimmung im Reitsport,* Müller Rüschlikon

11   Wolframm, I. (2012), *Dreamteam Pferd und Reiter: Persönlichkeitsbestimmung im Reitsport,* Müller Rüschlikon

As far as I'm concerned, it's like this: In order to be outstanding, riders need to know, deep down, right at their very core, who they are. In psychology circles, this is known as 'self-concept'. It's a kind of 'inner selfie', which is to say, the image people hold of themselves deep inside. What is more, riders need to have this kind of self-concept even before they've managed to achieve anything noteworthy in the realm of equestrian sports. In fact, they might only just have started riding, but they already *know* who they're meant to be. They already know they're meant to be *riders*.

So really, it boils down to just this: if you want to make it to the top, you need to be one hundred percent certain that there's nothing else you should be doing – even though you might still be as far away from the top as you are to the moon. And the icing on the cake is the unflinching, unwavering, unstoppable belief that you're capable of getting there, no matter the cost or how long it'll take. Just like Charlotte who took every opportunity to pursue her dream. Just like Kyra wouldn't be deterred by fear or a country that couldn't support her at the time.

I can almost see you shake your head in disbelief or even frustration.

How, I hear you ask, could anyone possibly believe they're anything – let alone something as ambitious as being a top rider – before they've gone out and done it successfully? How can a young girl's dream of becoming an Olympic Champion be anything more than a fervent wish? How can fantasy turn into reality with nothing more than a strong sense of self?

Here's the funny thing. It's not only possible, but it's actually really rather common among top riders (or those that are on the brink of it).

Take Emily King, eighteen-year old daughter to eventing supremo Mary King. In her own words:

'I was competitive from the start and always wanted to show her (Emily's mother, Mary King, ed.) *what I could do.'* [12]

There was clearly no doubt in this determined young lady's mind about what she wanted to do and she set about doing just that. At the

---

12   Stafford, C. (2014), 'Emily King', *Horse Sport International*, Issue 3

tender age of twelve, she accompanied her mother to the CCI4* event at Pau, France. At a young event horse sale, a grey caught her eye. When her mother declined to buy the horse for her, Emily took the initiative and sent a text to one of Mary's horse owners asking them to buy the horse for her. They agreed, and 'Timmy' was hers.

Six years later and Emily has competed at four European Championships, with an individual silver medal to her name. With a string of six event horses, she is working hard towards carving out her future in the sport.

To the cynics among you, it might be tempting to dismiss such a story with a shrug and a 'but she already had plenty of opportunity with Mary King as her mother'. Yet the moral of the story is an entirely different one. Even at a young age, Emily King knew precisely what she wanted to do – well before she'd ever done any of it, let alone started being successful at it. She considered herself an eventer years before she could conceivably call herself that. The belief in herself was so pronounced, so unshakable, she tried everything to make it happen. The further she travelled along the road towards turning her dream into reality, the more it reinforced her initial perception of herself as an event rider.

Charlotte Dujardin, our fairy tale princess of modern dressage is no different. Long before ever having competed internationally, she knew she really wanted to ride at the Olympics. It was her dream, her goal, her aspiration. It will have already started to shape who she was. The fact that she wasn't a top level dressage rider, let alone having ridden at advanced level yet didn't matter. Then, suddenly, an opportunity presented itself (or rather, she made it happen by asking Carl for lessons). It fitted right into the self-concept she had held of herself for so many years. Now, all she needed to do was take hold of that opportunity – just as Emily did when she sent that fateful text and received a positive answer.

But Emily King and Charlotte Dujardin are just two examples of many successful riders who accepted what was offered to them without a second thought, prepared to do anything to turn opportunity into success, quite simply because it matched precisely who they thought they were.

There are many other exceedingly well-known riders, who, like Emily and Charlotte, knew who they were meant to be from a very early age.

Take Carl Hester, Charlotte's mentor:

'I can't remember when it started, and there is no reason I can put a finger on as to why it did, but I was always fascinated by horses and ponies.' [13]

His sentiments are echoed almost word for word by Mary King, whose own parents weren't all that keen on horses. (At least not initially. Later on, Mary's mum would end up driving her around to shows in their old lorry):

'My mother, who was frightened of horses, had given up after three lessons. However, I was absolutely fascinated by them, and would spend hours sitting on gates staring at horses in fields.' [14]

So how about yourself then? Can you empathise with the early experiences of Emily, Charlotte, Carl or Mary, well before they were equestrian superstars? If you can, if you, too, have always had the sense that riding and being around horses is an integral part of who you are, it's an important foundation towards turning into the person you want to be.

But no matter how or why an innate connection to horses develops, it needs to be honed and developed as time goes on, to the point where it fuses into a 'rider persona' that ends up dictating the majority of riders' actions, decisions and life choices. As time goes on, sporting achievements follow (quite simply because these riders did everything they needed to in order to become who they wanted to be). These achievements in turn will help all riders, including you, grow even further into their own role. Then, finally, after years of successful participation in the sport, they might even develop into living equestrian legends – through sporting achievement but also through the image they portray outwardly and, more importantly, to themselves.

---

13   Hester, C. (2014), *Making it Happen*, London, Orion Books

14   King, M. (2009), *The Autobiography*, London, Orion Books

The educational psychologist Professor Dr Herb Marsh from Oxford University calls this phenomenon the reciprocal affects model, whereby an existing self-concept shapes achievement, and achievement shapes self-concept in turn. Marsh investigated this effect in great detail in the context of academics[15] , but other researchers have since determined its viability in a sporting context.

Let's take a closer look at how this might work in practice.

Most of us can readily believe that if we're good at something, it'll shape the way we see ourselves. However, it's the other way round that seems somewhat more complicated…

You see, it's like this: Every single human being possesses a self-concept, e.g. an image of what they believe they are like. For most of us, our self-concept is composed of several different roles we play as part of our daily lives. These are called 'self-aspects' and they can be many and varied.

You are a daughter or a son to your parents, a mother or father to your children, a husband or wife to your spouse. You are a friend, a colleague, a boss. You are a lawyer, a doctor, a bus driver, a clerk, or a teacher. You are also a rider. A dressage rider, a show jumper, an eventer, a vaulter, an endurance rider, a recreational rider, a horseman or woman.

Most importantly, each and every one of these self-aspects is characterised by different sets of attributes, depending on how we see ourselves in each of these different roles. For example, you might consider yourself a supportive, authoritative, empathetic parent, a loving, faithful spouse, and a competent, motivated rider (whatever your discipline). You'll no doubt have noticed that I've only chosen to use positive attributes in the description of those various roles, i.e. your self-aspects. Yet most of us will also have certain negative beliefs about ourselves. At times, we might also be impatient parents, ungrateful children, needy spouses or unavailable friends.

Some people compartmentalise these different negative and positive attributes into separate self-aspects. They might consider themselves a

15   Marsh, H. W., and Craven, R. G. (2006), 'Reciprocal effects of self-concept and performance from a multi-dimensional perspective: Beyond seductive pleasure and unidimensional perspectives. *Perspectives on Psychological Science*, pp. 1, 133-163

'competent, motivated' rider in training (only positive attributes) but in competition, they believe themselves to be 'easily distracted and highly nervous' (only negative attributes). The problem with such a compartmentalised view of the self is that the minute you enter a situation that invokes a negative self-aspect of yourself, you have no positive attributes to draw on to help you cope. If you enter a stressful competition, convinced that you are going to be distracted and nervous, it'll take a miracle for you *not* to be distracted and nervous. I hope you can see how such a negative self-aspect is going to be detrimental to your performance.

Much better, therefore, to integrate your positive and your negative attributes. Instead of separating your 'rider in training persona' from your 'competitive rider persona', you merge them into one. You'll view yourself as a competent, motivated rider, who sometimes struggles to concentrate and loses confidence. An integrated view of yourself means you'll have to admit to yourself that, even in your daily dealings with your horse, you're not perfect. However, it also means that you always have your positive attributes to draw on, even when things get a bit rough. There might be times, at a show (or any other stressful horsey situation) that you'll start to feel nervous. But now that you've integrated both negative and positive aspects, you'll have your motivation to draw on. Suddenly, you'll be able to remind yourself what it is you love about riding and what it is that keeps you going – regardless of whether you're at home in training or at a show ready to compete.

What is more, you can also draw on the positive attributes you hold in some of your other self-aspects. If, for example, you consider yourself a 'tough negotiator' at work, why not use that particular attribute to bolster your confidence in training? If you think you have the patience of a saint when dealing with your children or your husband, why not allow that particular attribute of yourself to boost your rider persona when tackling a particularly tricky training situation? Once you have integrated your various attributes into your 'rider self-aspect', it'll give you a buffer that'll help you when things get tough. It'll help you to believe in your own abilities, even when it seems that the odds aren't in your favour.

Needless to say that your rider persona should contain a number of positive attributes right from the word go.

Such as 'loving' the sport à la Charlotte Dujardin.

Such as being 'competitive' and 'wanting to show what I can do' à la Emily King.

Such as being 'fascinated by horses' à la Carl Hester.

But make sure you also allow certain negative attributes (the ones we all have about ourselves) to infiltrate your rider self-aspect. Don't lock them up in a separate self-aspect (such as a 'panicky competitive self') that only rears its ugly head when you least want it to. If you've got both negative and positive attributes assembled together in your one 'rider persona', the positive bits will help protect against insecurity and self-doubt in times of stress.

What is more, acknowledging – and integrating – unflattering characteristics of yourself into who you are as a rider will actually help you strive for improvement more effectively. Because now you'll finally have to confront those niggling issues. Since they've become part of the 'everyday you', you won't be able to stick your head in the sand any longer. If you want to become the best you can be, you'll have to address them.

But seeing that you've integrated the bad bits with the good, you'll be able to use your positive attributes as the driving force to help you overcome anything that has held you back in the past. As a result, your self-concept will grow more robust, more resistant to the obstacles that are likely to pop up along the way. And the more robust your self-concept as a rider (whatever kind of rider you want to be), the stronger the belief in yourself. Then, in the words of Carl Hester, you'll be able to 'make it happen'.

But don't just take my word for it. Look at how twenty-year old American Lucy Davis managed to beat all the Big Boys (and girls) of show jumping in one of the toughest competitions there is, the Final Grand Prix of the Global Champions Tour.

In the aftermath of her spectacular win against the world's elite in Lausanne in 2013, this plucky young lady said:

'I thought I had a chance. I wasn't sure if it was a serious chance because my horse is inexperienced, but when you're up against riders of this level you have to take a chance to win.' [16]

The short statement says it all. Lucy thought she had a chance. She believed in her own competence as a rider – regardless of the relative inexperience of herself and her horse (which might arguably be construed as negative attributes). In the end, none of it mattered because she was able to draw on the most positive attribute of them all: the belief that she could do it.

---

16   Longines Global Champions Tour, (2013), *Horse Sport International*, Issue 6

CHAPTER 2

DEFINING YOUR OWN SUCCESS

'Isabell Werth sets new world record score'
(*Horse & Hound* online, 21/11/2005)

'Anky extends own world record'
(*Horse & Hound* online, 27/03/2006)

'Moorlands Totilas breaks world record again
at Windsor Europeans'
(*Horse & Hound* online, 30/08/2009)

'Charlotte Dujardin and Valegro break world record in Germany'
(*Horse & Hound* online, 29/04/2012)

'Dujardin Conquers 2013 CDI-W London
with Kur World Record'
(*eurodressage*, 12/18/2013)

'Dujardin does it again with new world record score
in Reem Acra final Grand Prix'
(FEI, 19/04/2014)

The headlines say it all. We live (and ride) in a world where one record score chases the next. It's not just at international shows either – even at local, regional or national level there's a focus on 'highest score of the day', 'the week' or 'the competition'. What is more, due to the ever-present social media, it's become almost impossible not to know about it.

So, being a competitive rider striving for some level of recognition, some small measure of success, is tough. Perhaps tougher than ever before. Therefore, you and many other riders tell yourself that in order to be successful, you really should win.

Shouldn't you?!

So you put pressure on yourself – day after day.

You might not even realise it, but deep down you're convinced that if you really want to make your mark in the horsey world – be that at local or international level – you must win. Only then, you tell yourself, will you be able to emulate those modern equestrian legends. It'll be your name splashed across the front page of every equestrian magazine. You'll have thousands of Twitter and Facebook followers, and sponsors lining up to buy you a horse or ask you to endorse their products…

As the next show approaches, you've almost convinced yourself that you deserve to win. You've practised hard. You've got a good horse, you know your test. It's time you got your just reward! Then you get ready to leave for the show and all those thoughts are running wild in your head. So by the time you get to the show ground, you're wound up so tight nobody in your entourage dares to talk to you any more.

Then you find out who's judging today. Oh no! You're convinced that judge hates your horse. You'll never win now. But you must! You really, really, must. So you get on your horse. You manage to calm yourself, telling yourself how hard you've practised and that, surely, today it's going to be your turn.

You and your horse walk to the warm-up arena. Right there, heaven forbid, is your biggest adversary. What is she doing here? She rides that really expensive horse and her trainer's always by her side. That's not fair! You were going to win, and now you probably won't.

But you're here, so you might as well go through with it. You warm up your horse – keeping an eye on your nemesis the entire time. Her horse is more collected than yours, isn't it? And in the extended trot, her horse has got a lot more reach.

It's almost time to go in, and you try and make yourself focus on your horse. You rush through another few of the movements. They don't go all that well. Your horse feels less through than usual. But how can that be?

You've practised so hard… Never mind, you're in the ring now. Just before the judge (that dreaded judge – she isn't even smiling. Gosh, she really must hate your horse), rings the bell, you notice your old trainer (friend, owner of your horse, etc.) standing next to the enclosure, watching you. He's probably thinking your horse is going much worse than the last time he saw you. As if on cue your horse comes off your leg and sticks his nose in the air.

That's when the bell goes. You muddle through as best as you can. The final score is not great. You didn't win.

You go home. You're so disappointed.

Sound familiar? That's because almost every rider has fallen into this particular trap at one point or another. You, your mates at the yard, the riders down the road, just about anyone who ever wanted to be successful.

It seems so obvious. You want to be the best, so you focus on winning. You want to win, so you focus on beating everyone else.

The principle behind it all is called social comparison – comparing ourselves to the rest of the world.

As it happens, the Digital Age we currently live in is the ideal feeding ground for social comparisons. While it is of course fantastic that you can keep in touch with friends and family anywhere in the world, that you can follow news and watch history in the making without even getting out of bed, you are also continuously confronted with – and able to compare yourself to – what other people have, can and do.

The human race is innately competitive. We have to be, it's lodged deeply in our genetic make-up. After all, our chance at surviving and procreating, and thus ensuring our DNA lives on long after our bodies are done fertilising the cemetery, increases exponentially if we are bigger, stronger, smarter, prettier and better than anyone else. To the cavemen in us, being better is very attractive. It means ensuring the survival of our genetic heritage.

The ethologist and evolutionary biologist Richard Dawkins[17] developed the term 'classical fitness' to describe how 'fit' individuals are in

---

17   Richard Dawkins caused a furore with his book *The Selfish Gene*, published in 1990 by Oxford University Press.

terms of survival and producing offspring. From an evolutionary perspective, human beings strive to be 'fit', with 'fitter' automatically being associated with 'better'. It's like a software program working away in the background, regulating the things we do and think without us even realising. As a result we want to – no, we *must* – be the best, come what may.

But even though this innate competitiveness and tendency for social comparison can occasionally serve a purpose, in the context of equestrian sports it can be downright dangerous, as it is likely to have a serious effect on your frame of mind and subsequent ability to perform.

What now?

Simple, really.

All you need to do is reprogram that software in your head…

Throughout the 1980s, while working at the University of Michigan, the psychologist Thomas Nicholls developed his goal perspective theory, which has since been expanded on by several other researchers. The theory describes two opposing types of goal orientation: task versus ego orientation (which has also been referred to as mastery vs. competitive goal orientation). Individuals who are task (or mastery) orientated define success through personal improvement. They strongly believe that improvement is down to effort and persistence. As a result, they are inclined to participate in challenging situations, that allow them to 'stretch themselves'.

On the other hand, ego (or competitive) goal orientation stipulates that ability is independent of effort. The definition of success is outperforming other individuals without expending much effort, thereby demonstrating tremendous ability. Admittedly, there are times that ego-orientated individuals who seem to be 'on a roll' outperform their fellow competitors time and again, thus seemingly proving that their definition of success is the only viable one. But even a situation that, at first glance, appears so utterly desirable, can – and often will – have a very bitter aftertaste.

At the turn of the century, Richard Dunwoody was the most successful jump jockey in the history of National Hunt racing in Great Britain. From a total of 9,399 rides he won 1,699 times. That's a strike rate of 18 per cent! He was crowned champion jockey in terms of winners ridden and money earned several times over and was voted National

Hunt Jockey of the Year by his fellow jockeys five times. Clearly, Richard Dunwoody was a rider who knew a thing or two about winning. And yet, by his own admission, by the end of the season that earned him his last champion jockey title (1994–1995), he had grown very tired of the racing equivalent to the rat race:

> *'I was disillusioned with that chase. My marriage had gone, my reason was going and, to save my career, I had to regain control of my life. (…) Being champion jockey would no longer be the goal.'* [18]

But what happens if you're not in quite the same league as the Richard Dunwoodys of this world? What if you're not crowned champion over and over again? What if, one week, somebody else wins? And you come at the bottom of the pile. And again the following week. And again. And again. If you are purely ego-orientated – either through desperately trying to show your worth by winning or trying your hardest to avoid making a fool of yourself – I guarantee that you will struggle to maintain the motivation, let alone the focus and effort to keep going.

Incidentally, ego-orientation doesn't necessarily have to manifest itself in the relentless drive to win. Some people simply try their very best to avoid failure. Tony McCoy, who not only managed to match, but eventually supersede Richard Dunwoody in terms of winners ridden, admits to falling foul of this all-encompassing desire to avoid failure. In the early days of his career he was actually more concerned that he might *not* end up champion than with becoming champion[19].

To many riders, fear of failure, of not doing well compared to their peers, can be a fate almost worse than death. Their ego is on the line. In order to protect it and to avoid making a fool of themselves, they might even prefer not to compete at all – or only if they can be absolutely, 100 per cent certain they'll win.

---

18 Dunwoody, R. (2000), *Obsessed, The Autobiography*, London, Headline Book Publishing

19 McCoy, A. P. (2011), *My Autobiography*, London, Orion Books

By now you've probably realised that this form of negative perfectionism will quickly wear down almost any individual.

If, however, riders adopt a task-motivated approach, they are much more likely to see this as just another challenge to improve other aspects of their skill repertoire. Instead of giving in, they'll be likely simply to put in more effort.

In practice, this means the following: by focusing on winning (and thereby adopting an 'ego' or 'competitive' goal orientation), you're defining yourself and your ability through the performance of others. You've put yourself in a situation that is virtually impossible to influence, let alone control. There are simply too many variables you have no sway over: the judge, other riders, the horses other riders sit on. There's simply no way of knowing whether a judge might have had a fight with his/her partner in the morning, is just a teensy bit grumpy and therefore, if torn between a 6 and a 7, goes for the 6. You haven't got a clue how much money fellow competitors have invested in their horses, the kind of help they receive at home or whether their trainer schools their horse, and they only get on for a show. There's a whole host of unknown quantities that make it impossible to work out an appropriate competition strategy. If your only focus is on winning, you'll tie yourself in knots thinking about all the things you can't control: other riders, judges, spectators and so forth. The consequences are obvious: the moment you fail to concentrate on yourself and your horse, chances of your horse doing what he's supposed to be doing are pretty slim.

Instead, you need to try and 'reprogram' the software in your head and redefine what success means to you. Instead of saying 'I'm only successful once I win' you could ask instead 'How can I get better at riding my horse?' That way, you'll be able to focus on the things you *can* control: you and your horse. This, you guessed it, is 'task' or 'mastery' goal orientation. What is more, this is one of the key characteristics of top performers: wanting to get better. Every day. Independent of what everyone else does. Improving yourself is what matters while beating others becomes a by-product and an afterthought.

But don't just take my word for it. In the run up to the 2012 World Cup Final, in which she was considered the favourite, Adelinde Cornelissen shared her definition of success:

'Most importantly, I ride for myself. I ride because I enjoy it so much and because I love performing together with my equine partner. Winning really isn't important. In fact, I use competition as a marker to see how far I have come in my training. Once I have everything under control at home, I want to find out if we can do the same thing somewhere else, in a different environment and under more difficult conditions.' [20]

Adelinde sums it up beautifully. The beauty of it is that no matter the level riders are competing at, they can apply the same principle to their own performance. By focusing on what really matters to them, external pressures hold little sway. Competitions, and even championships, become something to look forward to (rather than something to be afraid of): a chance to see how far the training has progressed and how much the relationship with their horse has grown.

Much better therefore to shift your mindset from wanting to win to riding the very best you possibly can. This means thinking about all the things you can do to make sure your test really sparkles: solid practice, good management, leaving on time, knowing how to ride your warm-up, and, most importantly, knowing how you need to ride (all the things you do at home to get your horse on the aids, moving through the body, relaxed, forward, with plenty of impulsion, etc.).

Task (or mastery) orientation helps to turn a challenge into an opportunity! The essence of this is captured in three of the most valuable lessons Kyra Kyrklund received from her father:

'The first is that some things you can influence. You should put all your energy into trying to do just that.

The second is that there are things you can't influence. Don't waste any energy on those.

---

20   Wolframm, I. (2012), 'Mind over Matter: How mental training can raise your game', *Horse Sport International*, Issue 2

The third and most important thing is to learn what you can and what you cannot change.' [21]

So, really, the only way to being successful is remembering what you want to do and how you are going to go about doing it. There's no point in trying to influence things that are out of your control. In equestrian terms this means figuring out the way you would like your horse to move and respond to you in a dressage test, show jumping course, across country, on a race track or in any other setting, rather than worrying about whether you are going to get winning scores. Keep focusing on what exactly you need to do to make sure you give your horse every chance of performing just the way you want him to. How do you need to sit? How strong does your aid have to be? What kind of energy level do you, as a rider, need?

These types of question allow you to define precisely what it is you want from a test, a course, a show – rather than second-guessing everyone else.

By the way, measuring how successful you were at the end of a show becomes refreshingly straightforward: did you feel what you wanted to feel? Did your horse move and respond in the way you wanted?

If the answer is no, you need to go back and analyse where you went wrong in your preparation.

If the answer is yes, you were, indeed, successful!

---

21   Wolframm, I. (2012), *Dreamteam Pferd und Reiter: Persönlichkeitsbestimmung im Reitsport,* Müller Rüschlikon

CHAPTER 3

COPING WITH ADVERSITY

'I hit the floor and heard a loud crack inside my head.' [22]

Nick Skelton

It's a sunny day in September 2000 at the Park Gate Horse Trials and the world of show jumping is in shock.

Nick Skelton has just fallen of his horse. Nick Skelton. The British show jumping legend.

According to the reports, he landed headfirst, breaking his neck in two places. The injury might just as easily have been fatal.

At first though, Nick never entertained the thought that a single fall could spell the end to his career. However, several months later and the injury still hadn't healed properly. Nick bit the bullet and went into early retirement.

Then, the impossible happened. He recovered sufficiently, that, in 2002, he was cleared to ride again. Nick returned to competition on Arko III, a stallion he had ridden as a youngster before his near-fatal fall. The rest, as they say, is history.

In 2004, Arko III carried his rider to victory in the British Open, the first of a successive string of international honours: competing first at the Athens, then at the Beijing Olympics, winning medals at European and World Championships, Nations Cups, World Cups and many other noteworthy events, culminating in a team gold in London 2012, for which he was awarded an OBE (Officer of the Order of the British Empire) by Queen Elizabeth II. Not bad for a man with a broken neck...

And yet, Nick Skelton's isn't the only inspirational story of tragedy turned on its head.

---

22   Kirkup, J. (2012), 'Nick Skelton: Spills and thrills of a defiant winner', *www.telegraph.co.uk*, 6th August 2012

As an Olympic dressage rider with many successes at the top level to her name, Courtney King-Dye had everything going for her. A yard full of talented horses, plenty of ability and a thirst to become the best she could possibly be, the young American was living her childhood dream. Then, in March 2010, her life was suddenly turned upside down.

Courtney was schooling a six-year old, when the horse tripped and fell, trapping his rider underneath him. Courtney was not wearing a helmet and suffered a skull fracture and a traumatic brain injury, that left her in a coma for four weeks and unable to do the simplest of physical tasks for many months after. While her cognitive abilities were not affected, walking, talking, and, of course, riding, had turned into the ultimate challenge.

By April 2012 Courtney had recovered sufficiently to qualify for the US Paralympic Selection trial and earning her the 2012 FEI 'against all odds award'. She ended up not participating as her horse, Make Lemonade, was deemed unsuitable as a therapy horse. Undeterred, she now continues to ride, compete, teach, write, and, of course, inspire.

While Courtney King-Dye and Nick Skelton are extremes, many, if not most, well-known riders have had to overcome some kind of personal tragedy, seemingly insurmountable obstacles, problems that appeared too all-consuming to fix at some point or other in their career.

Think, for example, of Ludger Beerbaum. An exceptional show jumper, he never had a problem getting horses to perform. Until he took over the ride on Ratina Z…

Even though the mare had achieved a silver medal at the Barcelona Olympics under her previous rider, Piet Raymakers, she simply refused to show what she was capable of in the first few weeks of her time with Beerbaum. An almost traumatic experience for a rider, who, in show jumping circles is known as a perfectionist! Not to be deterred however, Beerbaum spent weeks looking for a solution. Eventually, after a complete rethink of the manner in which Beerbaum rode the mare, Ratina Z developed into one of the world's greatest show jumpers.

Then there's Edward Gal, who lost the ride on Moorlands Totilas after the pair's gold medal at the World Championships in 2010. The black phenomenon was sold to Paul Schockemöhle for an undisclosed sum. Despite the obvious heartache, Gal didn't grieve for long. He's back at the very top with another black pearl: Glock's Undercover.

Is it coincidence that Skelton, King-Dye, Beerbaum, Gal and many more like them emerged from their traumatic experiences seemingly stronger than before?

No. Of course it isn't.

Getting through tough times, successfully fighting their own demons, not allowing the rough stuff in (horsey) life to get them down or hold them back are the hallmarks of real survivors – and future champions. As these riders learned to cope with their lot in life, they developed vital coping skills that would stand them in good stead in future.

A career in sports – and especially in horse sports – is never going to be straightforward. We've already discussed the impossibility of trying to control all the variables on a single day of competition. Now imagine all the variables, factors, circumstances that have to come together to make a life in sport happen. For every one that works in a rider's favour, there are probably three more that'll work against her. For every horse that performs, there'll be three others that won't. Or there'll be an owner who decides to sell a horse. Or a sponsoring contract that won't be renewed. Or a groom who's suddenly quit. Or an old back injury that's suddenly flared up again. Or a lorry that breaks down and costs too much to fix.

The possibilities are endless, and yet they'll happen to just about any rider at some point or other in their career. And that's without taking into account all the things that might go wrong during actual competitions…

But if riders happen to have had some practice at managing situations that seemed unmanageable, of solving a puzzle that seemed unsolvable, many of the daily problems become minor blips. While annoying, they won't be enough to slow them down, let alone stop them from pursuing their real dreams.

Professor Dave Collins and Dr Áine MacNamara from the Institute of Coaching and Performance at the University of Central Lancashire, UK, suggest that overcoming trauma is an important precursor to top performances. In fact, studies have even identified certain traumatic stressors common in different types of sport. For example, proportionately more top footballers seemed to have been raised by a single parent, while an above average number of high-level rowers attended boarding school (considered a source of early trauma). By simply having to cope, it seems, these footballers and rowers developed skills necessary to deal with many of the difficulties a life in sport would throw at them later. They developed coping skills that could be used effectively across all types of situations.[23]

Incidentally, this idea that coping can be learned has also been shown by schemes such as 'Stress Inoculation Training' by Meichenbaum, or Rosenbaum's 'Learned Resourcefulness'. As participants were taught relevant coping behaviours, they showed much more resilience later on, when faced with real-life stressors.

So where does all of this leave you? I bet there've been quite a few instances in your own equestrian career that have been less than fun. Rather than enjoyable, motivating, and empowering, your chosen pastime has felt forbidding, thankless or even dangerous. You might have continually ended up near the bottom of the pile at competitions, or kept having disagreements with your horse that you didn't know how to resolve. You might have had to manage an endless stream of injuries – your own or that of your horse – and, unless you're exceedingly lucky, there will have been times when you've struggled to make ends meet.

It's a lot to deal with by anyone's standard. The question is, how do you cope? How does anyone?

Researchers in (sport) psychology agree that there are various ways of dealing with problems, but which particular manner we choose really depends on the situation we find ourselves in and how we've dealt with things in the past. According to Professor Mark Anshel[24] from Middle Tennessee State University, coping can be divided, on the one hand, into two styles, i.e. approach- or avoidance-styles, and, on the other hand, into two coping strategies, i.e. emotion- or problem-focused.

As the names suggest, an individual choosing approach coping aims

---

23   Collins, D., and MacNamara, A. (2012), 'The Rocky Road to the Top – Why Talent Needs Trauma', *Sports Medicine*, pp. 42 (11), 907-914

24   Anshel, M. H. (1990), 'Toward validation of a model for coping with acute stress in sport' *International Journal of Sport Psychology*, pp. 21, 58-83

     Anshel, M. H., and Wells, B. (2000), 'Sources of acute stress and coping styles in competitive sport', *Anxiety, Stress and Coping*, pp. 13, 1-26 to face the problem head on, while avoidance coping means temporarily sticking one's head in the proverbial sand. Problem-focused strategies are action orientated, that usually involve some kind of cognitive element too. Emotion-focused strategies deal with the feelings a problem has evoked. This leaves us with four coping measures to choose from:

	Approach coping style	Avoidance coping style
Problem-focused strategy	Analyse reasons for failures/difficulties and develop relevant solutions	Use mental or physical distractions
Emotion-focused strategy	Apply arousal regulation techniques, such as progressive relaxation or breathing exercises	Vent anger, cry

So then, when should you employ which coping strategy? And are any of them more effective than others?

For starters, the general consensus is that both avoidance and approach styles can have their merits in the short term. Yet in the long term an approach style wins hands down.

The reason?

If you keep running away from a particular problem, chances are, it'll keep coming after you. You end up never dealing with the problem, but merely shunting it to the back of your mind (where it'll continue to fester). If, however, you decide to face your problem, try and come to grips with it, you're much more likely to develop strategies that either reduce or eliminate it altogether.

Still, several studies have shown that elite athletes ranging from Olympic wrestlers to figure skaters are all able to pick and choose appropriate means of coping depending on the situation at hand[25]. In essence, this means that it's useful to acquire a proverbial 'kit bag' full of different coping mechanisms. All you have to do then is dip into it and fish out the style or strategy that suits your purposes. So let's have a look at how you might be able to use all of the available coping mechanisms to best effect.

Do you remember the incident of the 'Lost Gold Medal' for Bettina Hoy and the German event team during the Athens Olympics in 2004? It was the final show jumping day and Hoy had just commenced her show jumping round for the team medal. She crossed the starting line once, circled[26]… and crossed it again. A technicality that was to cost her – and the German team – the gold medal.

At the time, though, Bettina had absolutely no idea what had happened. The stadium clock had been reset, so she was unaware that her time had already started. She took her time completing her round, and ended up being awarded 14 time penalties. Shortly afterwards the FEI appeals panel removed the penalties, and, following a solid performance in the individual show jumping round, Hoy was awarded both the individual and team gold medals.

Then, a couple of days later, the Court of Arbitration for Sport decided that the FEI had no right to remove Hoy's time penalties – and belatedly awarded the team gold to France and the individual gold to the British rider Leslie Law.

Bettina Hoy's reactions to first winning and later losing the gold medal?

She cried. Both times. Who wouldn't have?

At the end of the day, *emotion-focused avoidance coping*, such as having a good cry, screaming into a scrunched up t-shirt, or stomping your feet like a five-year old can often feel extremely cathartic – for a little while at least. There are many who subscribe to the 'better out than in' school of thought, and if it helps to release pent-up tension, all the better.

---

25 Nicholls, A. R., and Polman, R. C. J. (2007), 'Coping in sport: A systematic review', *Journal of Sports Sciences*, pp. 25 (1), 11-31

26 At the 2004 Olympic Games, event riders had to jump twice, once for the team medal and once again for the individual placing

Most importantly though, your venting must never, ever be aimed at anyone else, particularly not your horse! Taking out your emotions on those around you, or even yourself, might be tempting, especially if you're looking for a scapegoat, but it'll cause more problems in the long run (a spouse or friend who's annoyed with you, a warning or suspension for abusing your horse, an incredibly guilty conscience for having allowed your temper to run away with you, etc.). Much better then, to take yourself away from the masses and vent in solitude.

But emotions are tricky. Sometimes they simply refuse to be kept at bay, especially if there's a lot at stake. So you'll need to tackle them head on. *Emotion-focused approach coping* can help to eliminate some of the physical symptoms that go hand in hand with emotional stress, or even distress. You might decide to go for a brisk walk or run. The release of endorphins caused by intensive exercise might help to settle you. But persuading your body to relax by applying techniques such as progressive muscle relaxation or abdominal breathing (see chapter 8 for more details) will also help your mind relax by association. Especially in horse sports, being in control of your body is of the utmost importance as it's the only way for you to communicate with your horse. Learning how to keep your emotions and your body in check can work wonders in your efforts to cope.

In terms of coping mechanisms, emotion-focused coping is possibly the most 'dangerous' style due to its potential to cause serious damage. On the other hand, if you know how to handle it appropriately, it'll give you a chance to release initial tension and then move on to more effective coping in a calmer state of mind. Bettina Hoy, for example, did just that. After the initial period of shock, she focused all her energy on her horses and came back stronger than ever before the following year, winning and being placed at some of the world's most prestigious events.

What about *problem-focused avoidance strategies* then?

Essentially, these are all about finding a distraction. Rather than examining, analysing or evaluating a problem, you force your mind to focus on something else, thus taking your mind off some of your worries, too. As a solution to a problem that is only short term, such as having to wait around until it's time to tack up, distracting yourself by playing games on your phone might just keep those pesky 'what if' scenarios at bay (i.e.

'What if the judge hates my horse?', 'What if everyone else is better than me?', 'What if I fall off and break my neck?'). In fact, in her autobiography, Pippa Funnell talks about playing computer games in the run up to the cross-country, precisely because she wants to avoid 'over-thinking' and fixating on her anxiety.[27]

It has probably become obvious by now that, especially in the long term at least, problem-focused avoidance is ineffective. After all, you cannot avoid your problems forever. However, even in the short term distractions must not end up being too distracting…

Especially in horse sports, once you get on the horse you need to be one hundred per cent attentive to what's going on underneath you. If you are still stuck in 'distraction mode', you might miss subtle cues from your horse – potentially resulting in much more obvious cues that could leave you watching the scene from a prime spot on the ground. Just make sure you remain aware of what you're doing and why you're doing it. Distraction is fine for a little while, as long as you know when you have to reemerge and face the world, your horse, and the situation head on.

So if *problem-focused avoidance coping* offers relief only in the short term, problem-focused approach coping becomes the obvious option for dealing with problems, issues, and challenges in the long term. In an interview with *Horse Sport International*, one of eventing's all-time greats, Sir Mark Todd, describes the approach of the Kiwi eventing team to securing a medal at the next championships, the World Equestrian Games in 2014.

'We have to target who we've got to beat and at the moment it's the Germans. (…) They leave nothing to chance. That's what our management team tried to do – have everything covered.' [28]

This is problem-focused approach coping par excellence:

---

27   Funnell, P. (2005), *The Autobiography*, London, Orion Books

28   Faurie, B. (2013), 'Knight of the Laid Back Order', *Horse Sport International*, Issue 4

1. Identify the problem (beating the Germans)

2. Analyse why success has been elusive so far (the Germans apparently leave nothing to chance)

3. Come up with a solution (have everything covered).

It's simple, yes. But it's very effective.

Solution-focused approach coping demands an analytical approach, driven by brains and the willingness to look closely at your own (and your horse's) strengths and weaknesses. In many ways, that's probably the most difficult part of approach coping. You need to be honest, and honesty can be tough (much more comfortable to try and ignore the problem and hope it goes away – which of course it won't). But once you've faced your inner demons, the potential for true growth is tremendous. Once you've identified what you can do to overcome a problem, there's little stopping you. I hope you can see why, in terms of longevity, problem-focused approach coping is the way forward.

You'll know this, of course, but allow me to reiterate anyway.

As riders, we continually deal with an animal approximately ten times as heavy as we are, with a will of its own. Sticking your head in the sand for longer than absolutely necessary is likely to make things much, much worse. Better to figure out a strategy of how to overcome a particular problem – even if, at times, you feel like a plaything of the elements without even one iota of control.

But take heart! There's almost always something you can do to at least change the situation for yourself. You won't be able to change how fellow competitors ride, nor how much money they spend on their horses. You also won't be able to influence how course builders assemble their tracks, nor the starting order of a competition.

There are, however, plenty of things you *can* do, such as ensuring you and your horse are physically and mentally fit and ready for the job in hand. Or getting your horse checked out regularly by a vet to prevent overuse injuries. You might want to take the time to develop a solid management programme for yourself and your horse. Or book regular lessons from a good coach (even if you're already an advanced rider – things do look different from the ground). Make sure you invest in good, safe kit for yourself and your horse. Lastly, keep an open mind and try to pick up new skills, such as relaxation techniques (always a good one to improve fine motor skills.)

The overriding message contained in all of this? Learning how to apply positive, situation-specific coping skills takes time. But it's time exceedingly well spent. Once you've developed a 'tool-kit' of coping skills, it (almost) doesn't matter what the horsey life throws at you, you can be pretty sure that you'll come out the other end better, stronger and more prepared!

CHAPTER 4

STAYING COMMITTED

'In anything in which you want to be successful, you have to be willing to work hard. It takes a lot of long hours and perseverance. It doesn't come overnight.' [29]

Margie Goldstein-Engle

Margie Goldstein-Engle (1958) is an American show jumping Olympian and a ten-time winner of the American Grand Prix Association Rider of the Year award. In 2011, she was the all-time career leader in Grand Prix wins, record holder of most Grand Prix wins in a single season (11), and two Grand Prix victories in two days. She was the first rider to have six (!) horses placed in the same Grand Prix and the first to be placed first through to fifth in a Grand Prix. And yet – it is not this, admittedly highly impressive, list of achievements that marks her as one of the all-time greats in equestrian sports. In fact, it's the things that happened in between winning classes that make her a shining example of being truly committed to horse sports.

But let's start at the beginning… As is the bane of many young riders, whether they go on to ride at top level or prefer recreational riding, Margie's parents were neither horsey nor particularly affluent. So, like all those other equally afflicted peers, young Margie mucked out stables and dog kennels in order to be able to afford more than one riding lesson a week. But while such commitment can be found in many passionate young riders, Margie didn't stop there. First of all, she wouldn't let her small stature stand in the way of her chosen career path. A little over five feet, she was told time and again, she should set her sights on a career as a race jockey – something Margie plainly didn't want. She wanted to be a show jumper…

---

29   Walton, R. (2013), 'In for the Long Haul', *Horse Sport International*, Issue 3

'I was more the height for being a jockey and they would try and push me in that direction. (…) I guess I felt like where there was a will there was a way. If you are willing to work at something hard enough, and you don't mind taking the downs, which are always going to be a part of this sport, with the ups, then you can make it.' [30]

And she made it alright – but at a price that someone less committed might perhaps not have been willing to pay. While competing in 1991, one of Margie's stallions fell on her crushing every bone in her foot. She was riding again the following day. In 1992, another horse fell on her, this time breaking her ribs and ripping open her back with the studs. In 1998, yet another horse tripped at a fence, resulting in Margie smashing her face. Once again, she got back in the saddle the following day. And these are not the only accidents or injuries Margie has had to endure. In fact, there've been so many, I wouldn't be surprised if she'd lost count!

The most amazing thing? Despite being plagued by accidents and injuries, Margie Goldstein-Engle was considered virtually unbeatable during that period. Every time she got knocked down, both figuratively and literally speaking, she managed to get back up again and rise like a phoenix from the ashes once more.

You'd be forgiven to for asking how on earth anyone might bring themselves to such levels of commitment. But the strangest thing is that Margie is definitely not the only example of a rider who sticks two fingers up at discomfort or pain (think Nick Skelton or Courtney King-Dye). More to the point, it seems to be yet another characteristic of riders on their way to the top.

We have already discussed the importance of being mentally 'tough', of redefining success so you are able to keep control, of being able to cope when things get tough, of knowing who you are and believing that, yes, you can! And then there's Margie Goldstein-Engle's (and a whole lot of other riders) refusal to give in or give up, demonstrating that there's yet another

---

30   Walton, R. (2013), 'In for the Long Haul', *Horse Sport International*, Issue 3

ingredient to the recipe of being truly successful – that of true commitment.

Imagine the following scenario. It's 6am on a Sunday in early February (or early August, if you happen to live in the southern hemisphere). The alarm clock's just gone off, and you're slowly coming to. As your senses adjust to the new day, you hear the snowstorm banging against your window. You wonder how you've managed to sleep through the racket in the first place… You're about to snuggle a little deeper into your warm and comfy covers, when realisation hits you. You've got to get up to feed the horses…

What do you do?

'Stupid question!' I hear you shout.

You get out of bed. Of course you do. There's no question about it. It's what makes you a horsey person. You might not particularly relish the thought of turning into a human icicle or being soaked all the way through to your underpants, but you'll do it. You'll do it because it's part of who you are, your self-concept, an important aspect of which includes being a rider. In turn, most riders define themselves by, amongst other thing, the dedication they feel to the animal(s) in their care. It motivates them to do whatever it is they have to do, day in, day out (with the odd day off thrown in for good measure).

This is likely to apply just as much to you as to any other dedicated rider. Over time, as you developed into the person you are today, you also developed the kind of attitude necessary for you to cope with entirely inhospitable conditions in order to look after your four-legged friends. The best, yet altogether weird, bit (at least if you're not a horsey person)? It feels perfectly natural. What is more, not being this committed would feel wrong.

That's why Margie Goldstein-Engle never would have seriously considered doing anything different, regardless of how many bones she broke. This kind of commitment is also the reason why Nick Skelton decided to make a comeback and Courtney King-Dye continues competing in para-dressage. One might be tempted to compare riders in general with red wine: they tend to improve with age.

Margie puts it like this:

'…I think once horses get in your blood, you almost get obsessed with it. (…) It's there for a lifetime.' [31]

I'd wager that this is a sentiment you'd wholeheartedly agree with. Loving horses – it's there for a lifetime. Once again, we're back to the topic of self-concept, of knowing who you are and what it entails. As long as that knowledge, that self-belief is strong enough, it doesn't matter what kind of obstacle horsey life throws in your way – you just get on and deal with it (using, hopefully, the most effective coping styles you can).

But there's more. And in many ways it goes hand-in-hand with knowing who you are and who you want to be…

First of all, think back to a time (it might be recent, or it might be a very long time ago) when you were coerced into doing something you didn't want to do. This could have been anything from having to do homework, studying for an exam or being made to go on walks with the family when you were little, to being treated as the general dogsbody at work, having to do the housework all by yourself, etc…

Have something in mind, do you? Thought so!

Unfortunately, doing things we'd rather not be doing seems to be part and parcel of not only growing up but being a grown-up. Most importantly though, do you remember how you felt at the time? Resentful probably. Annoyed or even angry. Listless perhaps. And, most definitely, neither motivated nor committed!

All of it seems to boil down to this: motivation and commitment are in no small part related to people's ability to control and influence the choices they make in life. Professors Edward Deci and Richard Ryan, both from the Department of Clinical and Social Sciences in Psychology at the University of Rochester, have spent theirs studying the underlying cause for why people behave the way they do. Their Self-Determination Theory (SDT) presents a broad framework that seeks to explain how environmental sources (such as social or cultural factors) and personality traits (such as individual determination or achievement striving) interact to improve well-

---

31   Walton, R. (2013), 'In for the Long Haul', *Horse Sport International*, Issue 3

being and performance. Most importantly, at the heart of SDT lies the premise that everyone, regardless of culture, gender or age, has an intrinsic need for autonomy, competence and relatedness.

Let's start with this concept of autonomy, which, I'm convinced, is central to any top rider. It describes people's need to influence their own destiny and to act in accordance with their self-concept. Autonomous individuals feel that their actions are congruent with their self-concept, and mirror the attributes they have given themselves. Their actions are their own and not determined by anyone or anything else. It's a sentiment Swiss show jumper and Olympic gold medallist Steve Guerdat feels very strongly about. When asked to describe what motivates him, he told *Horse Sport International*:

> 'I did it for me (before Olympic gold) and I keep doing it for me now. I don't try and think too much what other people expect from me.' [32]

Clearly one of the most autonomous riders out there, it seems that Steve has always made the choice that was right for *him*, rather than anyone else. In the three years leading up to 2006, he had climbed into the top of the World Rankings by the tender age of 26. However, after a disagreement with his boss, former Dutch Olympian and horse dealer extraordinaire, Jan Tops, Steve found himself horse- and income-less. Salvation beckoned in the form of owner Alexander Onishchenko, who was putting together a Ukrainian show-jumping team. It probably wouldn't be an exaggeration to call Onishchenko's set-up the equestrian equivalent of the land of milk and honey, with top horses, top facilities and top coaching available to the chosen few. Indeed, only a few months later, Onishchenko's team came very close to securing a bronze medal at the World Equestrian Games in Aachen.

Yet Steve wasn't to be part of it. The price, it turned out, was simply too high! When asked to sign a contract that would have turned him into

---

32   Lonnell, C. (2013), 'The Swiss Phoenix Rises', *Horse Sport International*, Issue 6

an Ukrainian overnight, the young Swiss realised he couldn't bear the thought of not listening to the Swiss national anthem being played at prize givings. Clearly, giving up his nationality would have felt too much like losing a hold on his destiny. So, for the second time in a few short months, Steve was without a job, without a horse, but still very much in control of his own future in the sport.

Even though he wouldn't have known it then, passing up what appeared to be a fantastic opportunity, paved the way for his future success. Back in Switzerland, Steve initially rode a few youngsters for friends, but soon after secured a sponsorship deal with the watchmaker Yves Piaget. A number of successful shows later, and multimillionaire Urs Schwarzenbach took the talented show jumper under his wing, offered him a base at his yard, and bought him the horse Nino du Buissonets, the horse that would carry him round the 2012 London Olympics – and win him the first Olympic medal for a Swiss rider since 1924. The horse that would allow him to listen to the Swiss – rather than Ukrainian – national anthem being played once again.

But as heart-warming as Steve Guerdat's story is, it also shows that acting autonomously can, at times, present an enormous challenge – especially if the expectations of others end up conflicting with a rider's own priorities, wishes and dreams. Again, Steve knows a thing or two about others' expectations:

> *'I hope it (winning the gold medal) hasn't changed me, but it has changed everything around me.'* [33]

While lucrative sponsorships deals (in Steve Guerdat's case with Honda and Rolex) are usually very welcome side effects of winning any kind of prestigious championship, they also bring with them many demands on a rider's time and effort. The pressure to perform, for the sponsors, the media, and adoring fans can become tough to handle. At times, it may feel only too easy to simply get swept away by such a tidal wave of popularity. It

---

33   Lonnell, C. (2013), 'The Swiss Phoenix Rises', *Horse Sport International*, Issue 6

might even be fun to be basking in the limelight for a while. Yet sooner or later, external demands may start to overshadow that feeling of autonomy that we now know lies at the centre of motivation.

Do you recognise yourself in any of this, even perhaps on a smaller scale? Do you sometimes run the risk of allowing the wishes and demands of those around you to dictate your choices and behaviour? Do you keep putting your own needs (and those of your horses) off in favour of everyone else's demands? Do you feel that you are filling your time with endless tasks that are only remotely connected to those that you'd like to be doing?

Then you might need to remind yourself who you are: your self-concept, self-aspects, positive and negative attributes, the works. Try and stand still by what matters most to you, and then decide whether you are still doing everything you need to live 'in congruence' with yourself. Try to determine whether your need for autonomy is still sufficiently met. If you feel that it is, all the better. If it's not, take action now!

But let's face it, all the autonomy and self-directed behaviour in the world isn't going to satisfy you completely if you're not getting better at whatever it is that you've set your mind and heart to do. According to Deci and Ryan's Self-Determination Theory, developing competence is another strong intrinsic human need. As they go through their lives, people try to master the world they've chosen to live in. What is more, they really want to be effective at it.

This desire to improve, to get better at their chosen occupation is clearly something that characterises every top equestrian. In order to reach the very top of your game, you need to want to learn, improve, get better every single day. Luckily, horses have been shown to be amazing teachers, responding with uncanny accuracy to every cue you give – or fail to give – them. And when you get it right, there's possibly no better feeling in the world, providing all the motivation you need – and then some!

In her autobiography Mary King describes how just such a moment made her feel… It's the 1996 Olympic Games in Atlanta, where Mary was competing as an individual. Even though these Games ended up fairly unspectacular for both the British (eventing) team and Mary herself, there was one particular incident that she describes with particular fondness – because it fulfilled her need for competence:

'Finally, it was our go. William (King William) did an amazing dressage test. He had an early draw, and felt soft and responsive, enabling me to ride him positively and elicit the very best of his impressive movement. The crowd went wild, Union Jacks flapped everywhere, and when I saw Annie (King William's owner), she was in floods of tears because she was so proud.

I received nines from all three judges for my riding and our overall score was 31, which was a terrific mark, possibly even a record for Olympic eventing. (...)

When I came out of the arena, the late Dr Reiner Klimke, an Olympic gold medallist in pure dressage and one of the most revered figures in the sport, said to me, "That was real dressage." It is still one of my most treasured compliments and was a very special moment.' [34]

I hope you can see why the incident would satisfy just about any rider's need for competence, including Mary's... For one, Mary experienced a truly amazing ride ('(he)...felt soft and responsive, enabling me to ride him positively'). This in itself is most of the time sufficient to help a rider feel competent and, as a result, motivated. I cannot stress it enough – horses are amazing instructors, providing riders with instantaneous and crystal clear feedback. The feel of a responsive horse is more than enough to let you know that you've done it 'right'.

But Mary also received external validation from not one, but two highly qualified external sources (the judges and Dr Reiner Klimke). While we discussed the need to define success within the remits of your own performance parameters (and I still hold by that), being told by someone you admire and whose opinion you value that you are a good rider will nevertheless help you believe in your own levels of competence... which, by the way, is exactly why so many riders are addicted to winning competitions.

34   King, M. (2009), *The Autobiography*, London, Orion Books

Coming first, being better than the rest, is one of the most obvious and immediate ways to feel competent. (The fact that it is a relative type of competence, as it is dependent on the performance of others is, unfortunately, all too often ignored in the endorphin-fuelled excitement of the moment.) Let's not forget, one of the attractions of participating in competition is the external validation of competence. Being told by a judge that you've done a good job, ending up on top of the podium, beating riders who you think are the bee's knees will make you feel, at least for that one moment, that you are competent, that you are a good rider, that all your hours training have been worthwhile – because somebody else has said it and because you've beaten all the other competitors. Incidentally, this is also why it's so terribly tempting to merely focus on those external sources. After all, it's much easier to believe someone else rather than your own, somewhat subjective, opinion…

But nobody is born an Olympic Champion (wouldn't that be nice!). Becoming competent is a lengthy process that will, quite frequently, involve lots of hard work, making mistakes and being set straight by those 'in the know'.

In his autobiography, Carl Hester describes in a charming and disarmingly honest manner what happened when he 'developed a fascination for dressage and getting horses "on the bit"'. He would get on his pony Spot-On and, by his own admission 'see-saw away on Spot-On's mouth until he would finally drop his head'[35] .

Clearly, the young Carl Hester had already figured out that being competent at dressage meant being able to ride a horse in an outline – so that's what he tried to do. The rebuke of one of his trainers in the form of 'Carl, less use of the hands, please'[36] might have been suitably embarrassing – but it would also have encouraged him to find other, more effective (and kinder) ways of achieving competence on horseback. The results of this quest are what we see today in the ring.

It is an important message for riders at any level. Achieving

---

35   Hester, C. (2014), *Making it Happen*, London, Orion Books

36   Hester, C. (2014), *Making it Happen*, London, Orion Books

competence takes time. I've already mentioned Ericsson's famous 10,000 hours that any top performer will have racked up by the time they reach the rank of expert. In horse sports, learning is a lifetime ambition, as every horse is different, and every day presents a new challenge. Be that as it may, making mistakes is definitely part and parcel of becoming a rider – and as long as you try and learn from those mistakes, they'll help you quell that innate need to improve. That is, at least temporarily, until you've realised that there's yet another level of competence out there and now you're set to achieve that too…

In essence then, being able to act autonomously, choosing your own path and trying to act in accordance with who you think you are, while also taking the necessary steps towards being competent at what you've set out to do, will ensure that you stay committed. For life.

Post script: 'Hang on!' I hear you cry out. 'You've forgotten to discuss relatedness!'

Ah yes! Well spotted.

We'll take a closer look at what relatedness means to people – and to riders – in much more detail in the next chapter.

CHAPTER 5

YOU'RE NOT ALONE

I think we can all agree by now that getting to the top is no walk in the park. While the highs might make you think you're standing on top of Mount Kilimanjaro, the lows will feel more like being pitched all the way down to the bottom of the Mariana Trench in the Pacific Ocean. That's almost twice as deep as Kilimanjaro is high.

More specifically, in order to get to the top, first of all, you'll have to face and overcome trauma. Despite – or because of – the trauma, you'll have to stay true to yourself and to your own desires while everyone else wants you to do something else. You'll have to continuously reexamine yourself for potential weaknesses, and then you'll have to work at fixing those, one weakness at a time. Throughout all of this, you'll have to try and not compare yourself to others, but stay in control of yourself, your training, your competition, your life.

And you'll have to do all of it on your own.

Right?

Err… no! Thank goodness.

Ever read the acknowledgement section of any – and I mean any – modern equestrian autobiography? Ever listened to or read an interview with a top rider after they've landed a big win? If they are decent human beings (which they are), they'll say something along the following lines:

'A lot of people have helped me to get this far.' [37]
Richard Dunwoody

'The list of people I would like to thank is endless: the vets who have helped and advised me over the years (...), my brilliant

---

37   Dunwoody, R. (2000), *Obsessed*, Headline Book Publishing

farrier; my owners and sponsors past and present on whom I am totally reliant (…). Thank you to all my hardworking grooms who I have had over the years – thank you for your part in helping me achieve my dreams.'[38]

Mary King

'During my thirty-five years, a great many people have been influential or have helped and supported me through the highs and lows and I am eternally grateful to them: (…).'[39]

Pippa Funnell

'A special thanks must go to all the people who have worked for me over the years to make my life with horses possible, and especially at the moment head girl Charlie Gardiner and my PA Becky Elvin who between them make sure that things run smoothly.'[40]

Sir Mark Todd

So then, even though getting to the top may be hard, you will not have to do it alone – and nor should you try! The 16th century English poet, John Donne, once put it like this:

'No man is an island.'

Professors Deci and Ryan, the brains behind Self-Determination Theory (see previous chapter), have a slightly more elaborate explanation. To them, the concept of relatedness is as important as being autonomous in your decisions and showing that you're competent. As human beings, it seems, we are innately driven to connect and engage with others. We want to care for them and want to experience being cared for in return.

---

38   King, M. (2009), *The Autobiography*, London, Orion Books

39   Funnell, P. (2005), *The Autobiography*, London, Orion Books

40   Todd, M. (2012), *Second Chance: The Autobiography*, London, Orion Books

The interaction with those around us can help us grow as individuals, or feel cherished just for the way we are. We learn to see things from a different perspective. That is because every person happens to have an individual, and thus unique, take on the world at large and their problems in particular. What is more, engaging with others may reveal new ways of coping. They might have resources at their disposal that we desperately need but can't provide ourselves, such as relevant knowledge (such as from a specialist trainer), emotional support (such as from a partner, best friend or even a mental coach), or something as mundane but undeniably important as financial backing (such as from an owner or sponsor).

By experiencing support from those around us, we will feel validated in who we are, and by extension, what we do. And while it is essentially up to you to decide who you want to be, the support of at least some significant others can only strengthen your resolve – and you know by now how important it is to believe – and keep believing – in yourself.

All the more important therefore for any ambitious rider (or parent of such a rider) to recognise that seeking support from others isn't a sign of weakness. Far from it. It's a sign of strength and commitment to who you want to be.

But here's the thing: first, you must want something, really want it, before you can go and get help on your way to achieving it. Support from others is driven by what you wish to achieve. The will and the inner drive comes first, the rest will follow – even if sometimes it feels like a really big coincidence – or a small miracle.

So then, let's take a look at some of those coincidences-cum-miracles that helped some of the world's top riders to get where they are today.

Let's be honest, there's probably no other moment quite as precious – nor the support from the people around you quite as important – as that very first time the fledgling rider feels that first spark of love for horses – a spark that, for some, will turn into a flame, hot and bright enough to sustain a lifetime of equestrian passion. But while there's no fire without a spark, you also need decent kindling. Decent kindling in the shape of support by parents, extended family or significant others.

And family support doesn't come much more obvious than that

enjoyed by British eventer Zara Phillips[41], fifteenth in line of succession to the British throne, and winner of the World Championships in 2006. Both her parents Anne, the Princess Royal, and Captain Mark Phillips, are accomplished equestrians themselves. Her mother won the European Eventing Championships in 1971 and competed in the 1976 Olympics, while her father won Badminton Horse Trials no less than four times. He now works as the Chef d'Equipe for the US eventing. Zara's grandmother, Queen Elizabeth II, has kept horses all her life, and has a particular fondness for owning and breeding racehorses, while her grandfather, Prince Philip remains the longest serving President of the FEI, the International Equestrian Federation. With all that much horse-sense around her, Zara couldn't have wished for a better start to her equestrian career. And you'll hardly be surprised to learn that the future World Champion started riding at the tender age of two and a half on a Shetland pony, given to her for Christmas.

Yet having 'horsey' parents and having the opportunity to ride from an early age is no guarantee for medals, not even for someone of royal blood! In addition to teaching Zara the necessary skills on horseback (something that Zara's father was more than qualified to do, of course), her parents also instilled in her the necessary mental attributes to succeed. The early days of Zara's equestrian career were apparently marked by a somewhat lackadaisical attitude, which Captain Mark Phillips was unwilling to tolerate. 'Is it easy? No.' He allegedly said to her. 'Is it tough? Yes.'[42] And yet, it was he who instilled in her one of the most important attitudes to becoming a world-class athlete and rider: determination.

All of this proves that even though a young rider – or any rider – might have many of the necessary prerequisites, they still need to be nurtured. While desires to be competent and make independent decisions are considered an innate human need, the necessary attributes don't develop by themselves. They need to be honed and fuelled, preferably by someone close by.

---

41 Married to former England rugby player Mike Tindall, Zara has kept her maiden name for professional occasions

42 From *Zara Phillips* by Brian Hoey, published by Virgin Books, reprinted by permission of The Random House Group

But while there are many, many champion riders who come from a horsey background – if perhaps not quite as privileged as that of Zara Phillips – there're many more, whose parents didn't know the first thing about horses.

Take British Olympic show jumper Tim Stockdale. By his own admission, when he was little, he 'didn't like riding because it hurt and [he] hated horses even more because they smelled funny and had minds of their own'[43]. Tim's parents were resolutely non-horsey. His father was a builder, while his mother stayed at home to look after Tim and his five siblings (four brothers, one sister). Yet, one day, when Tim and his twin brother Ivan wouldn't stop squabbling, their mother decided to take action and get them out from under her feet. She packed them into the car and drove them to the local riding school. At first, young Tim turned up his nose (quite literally) at the ponies there, preferring instead to carry out odd jobs around the farm. His 'reward' for his efforts, however, were to be riding lessons. Tim Stockdale was hooked after his first gallop – and things quickly evolved from there. When he got Danny Boy, his first pony, the lady selling him insisted that Tim also join the local Pony Club. Suddenly, a whole new world opened up for him. Suddenly, all his free time was spent training Danny Boy, reading *The Pony Club Manual of Horsemanship* (he called it his bible) and trying to absorb as much about how to look after his four-legged friends as possible. More importantly, his parents, despite not knowing anything about horses themselves, instilled in him an attitude towards his horses that would shape the way he treated them for the rest of his career.

'I can't ever remember missing a morning's ride and Dad would always make sure I took the ponies out for their morning constitutional. "If you have an animal, you can't leave it inside – it's cruel," Dad would say and he was right. Even now I still think it's cruel to keep a horse in its stable all day long.'[44]

43   Stockdale, T. (2012), *There's No Such Word as Can't*, Croydon, Tim Stockdale

44   Stockdale, T. (2012), *There's No Such Word as Can't*, Croydon, Tim Stockdale

More than that, Tim credits his exceptional equine management skills to the way he was brought up by his father.

> *'(…) I continued to read my Pony Club Manual from cover to cover. I never tired of it and loved reading about ponies, enthusiastically making up management charts and training programmes for my ponies, keeping a tab of our successes and failures, when and where things went wrong and why I thought they had in my very limited experience. In fact, this is something I've carried forward to my business today – I'm forever making lists, and like to plot and plan my horses' progress, and see at a glance how they're all doing. Of course, this organisation and planning was ingrained in me from a very early age by Dad, and it certainly helped that I am, by nature, a grafter.'*[45]

In addition to this being an excellent example of appropriate planning (which we'll discuss later on in the book), it also demonstrates the importance of the support we receive and the lessons we learn from the people surrounding us in those formative years. While for Zara Phillips her parents were of course ideally placed to instil in her the relevant knowledge and attitude, Tim Stockdale was helped on his way by a number of different individuals. So despite enjoying very different upbringings, the end results, one might say, are very similar. In fact, I'd even go as far as to argue that it doesn't even matter whether that initial push in the right direction and subsequent support comes from the parents, as long as

a) mum and dad are at least supportive in principle of their child's ambitions and foibles

b) there's someone (or several someones) who provide the right kind of incentive.

---

45   Stockdale, T. (2012), *There's No Such Word as Can't*, Croydon, Tim Stockdale

In the words of Carl Hester, who, as we've learned, is another example of a top rider emerging from an entirely non-horsey background:

'However, the fact that my parents were non-horsey, yet I was given the right direction by many people, that is hopefully an inspiration to those kids out there today who feel they can't afford to make it to the top professionally. I want to give them hope that they too can make it happen.' [46]

Early support is vital, that much is clear. But even though none of us can turn back time – nor choose a different family for that matter – there are still a number of lessons that we can draw from equestrian legends such as Zara Phillips, Tim Stockdale and Carl Hester (and many others just like them).

The need for support, for surrounding yourself with people who are prepared to stand by you no matter what, doesn't wane over time. In fact, the more competitive and professional you want to be as a rider, the greater your need for an extended 'horsey family', who will be there for you no matter what (incidentally, most of the time, your real family is likely to feature heavily in your horsey family, too). And just like any normal family, there'll be different roles for different members.

For starters, unless you're very wealthy yourself, you'll need help in financing your sport. Owners and sponsors become the obvious choice and establishing a solid relationship with them is key to continuity. We've all seen what happens when riders and horses get separated, Edward Gal and Totilas being the obvious case in point. [47]

At the start of 2014 it looked as if another successful Dutch combination might be torn apart in similar fashion: Gerco Schröder and the horse then known as Eurocommerce London. The dream duo won

---

46   Hester, C. (2014), *Making it Happen, The Autobiography*, London, Orion Books

47   It should be noted though that after three years together, the original wonder horse has really gelled with his new rider Matthias Alexander Rath. In many ways, the story of Rath having to live up and cope with the expectations of the entire dressage world is yet another excellent example of determination, perseverance and, above all, mental toughness

individual and team silver at the 2012 – how uncanny – London Olympic Games and racked up countless prizes at the top level of show jumping. Yet in late 2012, as the excitement of an Olympic medal was still fresh in everyone's memory, Ger Visser, head of Eurocommerce stables, declared personal bankruptcy and was subsequently taken to court for outstanding bills. Visser tried to sell all Eurocommerce horses, including London and several other top show jumpers, to his son, Ger Visser jr. A Dutch court put paid to the idea, and ordered all the horses to be auctioned off.

There'd be no telling where London would end up. A nightmare to any rider, and undoubtedly more than heart wrenching to Gerco. But sometimes miracles do happen.

Gaston Glock, founder of the Glock firearms emporium and generous sponsor of Dutch dressage riders Edward Gal and Hans-Peter Minderhout, stepped in just in time to prevent what one might call another 'Totilas incident'. He paid 8.6 million euros – not exactly the kind of money riders have lying around, I'd wager.

One could argue that Gerco would have continued to make his mark in the world of show jumping without his No. 1 horse. One could also argue that 'Glock's London' is rather on the pricey side and there're many more good horses that cost a fraction of that price. All true. But it doesn't even come close to being at the heart of the matter.

The point is, top riders need people like sponsors and owners. That way, there's one less thing to worry about and riders can focus on what they do best. Ride. So even if your name isn't Edward Gal, Hans-Peter Minderhoud or Gerco Schröder and your chances of being sponsored by Glock are minimal at best, don't be afraid to go out and find financial backing. Who knows, it might just be the beginning of your own personal fairy tale!

But once you've got one or several good horses, you'll still need to train and manage them, let alone plan the logistics of competitions. So until cloning becomes a real possibility, the ambitious rider will have to rely on faithful partners, assistant riders, and, of course, grooms. They are the backbone of any stable yard, responsible for the horses' welfare whether at a show or when the boss is away and the last buck generally stops with them. Take Jackie Potts. She's been head groom to British world-class eventer

William Fox-Pitt for twenty years – a testament to the loyalty she feels towards 'her' rider. To show his appreciation, in 2006 William nominated Jackie for the FEI Groom of the Year award – which she won with flying colours. In William's own words:

> *'Jackie and I have enjoyed twenty seasons together, there have been some amazing highs and terrible lows but through them all she has kept her feet firmly on the ground and her chin up. She is a huge support to me, always loyal and it is an absolute privilege to work with someone so dedicated and professional.'* [48]

And yet, riding, whether competitively or not, also means performing. You want to improve, get better, become the best you can be (it's that need for competence again). So you'll need people with additional expertise to help you get there. You'll need to put together your own professional support team: your trainer, vet, farrier, physio (for your horse and yourself), saddler, nutritionist, sport psych, etc. The list is, if not endless, potentially very long indeed. While you won't need them by your side all of the time, you must be able to rely on them, trust their opinion, and be prepared to follow their advice.

Don't be fooled, though.

It can take quite a while to come across an individual whose advice you're prepared to accept at face value. But it is worth devoting some time to finding the type of people you can truly relate to, as there may come a moment when your health or that of your horses depends on them.

Something Mary King can relate to…

It was in the spring of 2001 when the outbreak of foot-and-mouth disease in the UK caused the entire countryside, including equestrian events, to close up shop. Yet young event horses still need to be exercised, so Mary decided to take a young King George for a canter in a nearby field. Startled by a pheasant, the horse jumped to the side. Mary lost her balance, which scared the youngster even further. His subsequent and violent bucks

---

48   Fox-Pitt, W., and Clinch, M. (2007), *What Will Be*, London, Orion Books

caused one of the greatest event riders of the world to be thrown off and onto her head.

> *'I tried to get up, but, alarmingly, I couldn't lift my head off the ground.'* [49]

Mary comments in her autobiography. Alarming doesn't even cover it, as the hospital surgeon soon discovered a neck vertebra smashed to pieces. Only an ingenious operating procedure quite literally saved her neck – and her career. His advice on whether she would – or should – continue riding was simply that the risk of Mary hurting her neck again was minimal. More importantly, the ultimate deciding factor would be whether she could handle it mentally, not physically. As it was, the accident did not dent Mary's confidence. There is no doubt in my mind that, in part, this was due to the professional support and advice she received from her surgeon. He was able to relate to her, the passion and commitment she felt for her sport and helped her get through a particularly tough time. (Incidentally, the other part would have been the strength of Mary's self-concept.)

That is what 'relatedness' is. A human support structure composed of knowledge, skill and empathy that'll help you cope with whatever life throws at you.

If you still don't believe me, take a good look around at all the riders you admire and you'll find that none of them, neither man nor woman, is an island. You don't have to be either!

---

49   King, M. (2009), *The Autobiography*, London, Orion Books

CHAPTER 6

NO EXCUSES!

So here's a question for you: Have you ever felt utterly, completely committed to a project, a goal or an idea?

When inspiration first struck, you were convinced that nothing, absolutely nothing, could stop you. You were going to get there, and heaven help the poor soul who'd stand in your way. But then, a few days, weeks or months later, you're still pretty much exactly where you started. Right at the beginning.

Every time, it seems, you're about to get going on whatever you were so committed to, you end up doing something else. Sometimes there's a very good reason for it. In fact, there's a good reason for it every time. That's what you tell yourself, anyway.

Need me to be more specific, do you? All right, then. Here goes. Meet Juliette. She's finally decided to start competing again in dressage (but, really, it could be any discipline) after a break of almost four years. The horse she rode back then was very difficult, and most of the time, she ended up not getting very good scores. These days, she owns a talented six-year old. In the safety and security of the indoor arena at home, Juliette can get him going nicely. But about a year ago Juliette took him to his first show, where he got overly excited by the atmosphere, and she didn't get the scores she'd hoped for. She hasn't dared to take him out since.

Still, her trainer thinks that if Juliette was to take him places more regularly, he'd get used to being ridden elsewhere. Then, or so her trainer promises, they'll get the scores they are capable of. But Juliette is determined not to compete again until she's at least 110 per cent sure she can beat any other competitor in her class.

Admittedly, she could take the horse somewhere for training. But at the moment, things are really busy at work and she hardly has time for herself (even though, for some reason, she always ends up staying down at the yard for much longer than she'd planned).

Anyway, last Wednesday she did try and organise an outing to a yard nearby. Unfortunately she ended up having to work late and forgot to call the owners to cancel. She's tried to call again to reschedule, but they didn't pick up. Surely she can't be blamed for them not answering their phone?

Her partner offered to come with her to help her load and unload. That was a couple of weeks ago and he hasn't mentioned it since. Juliette reasons that he obviously didn't want to come with her in the first place. Not really, anyway. So she hasn't asked him again either, because if he really cared, he'd let her know when he's available.

Then, last week, her trainer called to tell her about a small unaffiliated show nearby. The perfect opportunity to practise. But Juliette had already promised her best friend's teenage daughter she could come and ride that day. Saying no would have been incredibly mean.

I don't need to go on, do I?

You probably already hate Juliette enough as it is, frustrated by her inability to get her act together.

In fact, Juliette is continuously inventing reasons as to why she cannot start tackling the biggest training issue with her horse, allowing her to postpone competing indefinitely.

This is called self-sabotage.

Unfortunately, Juliette is no exception when it comes to avoiding taking those first steps towards a goal. At some point, almost everyone engages in behaviours, thoughts, emotions or actions that prevent us from achieving the things we really want to achieve.

Still, you're probably asking yourself why on earth people would go out of their way to sabotage their own measure of success. After all, being competent, proving that you're good at whatever you set your sights on, is an intrinsic human need.

Right?

Right!

That's why self-sabotage is mostly a subconscious mechanism. Once it kicks in, you might be dimly aware of your behaviour, thoughts, actions or emotions, but you won't necessarily know why you're engaging in any of it. What is more – and here comes the tricky part – it'll feel like you're doing the right thing too.

The reason? Deep down, your conscious goals are in conflict with your unconscious desires or fears. Paradoxical? Not really.

Conscious goals might indeed be what you really, truly want in the long term. But if, in the back of your mind, you're harbouring strong short-term worries or needs, your overall behaviour will be guided by exactly those worries or needs. In essence then, self-sabotage is a protective mechanism trying to prevent you from experiencing (short-term) disappointment, getting hurt, losing face or indeed anything that might be considered traumatic.

In Juliette's case, the self-sabotaging behaviours, thoughts, and, let's face it, excuses she engages in, protect her from the potential disappointment of not doing well at a show. The longer she procrastinates, the longer she won't have to deal with the possibility that she's an incompetent rider – which is exactly how she felt with her previous horse. On top of all of that, Juliette's own brand of self-sabotage protects her from potentially getting hurt, if the horse really decides to play up again while away from home – which, in her eyes, might serve as another reminder that she's simply not very accomplished in the saddle.

In many ways, the status quo suits her just fine.

So you see, self-sabotage is all about helping you stay comfortable in the short term. But the thing is, in order to be truly successful, you need to feel *uncomfortable*. Once in a while, you need to venture towards the edge of your own limits.

It's what Susanne Lebek does. It's what she's always done. The German dressage rider won team and individual gold at the Junior European Championships in 1986, and, 13 years later, won bronze with the German team at the senior European Championships in Windsor, UK.

In equestrian circles, Susanne is well known for her talent to get the most out of 'difficult' horses. Horses that challenge her. Horses that test her to the limit. So far, she's been incredibly successful, managing to turn even the most difficult horse into a willing partner.

Her secret weapon? Dare to make mistakes, to perhaps even get stuck once in a while. There's something to be learned from every mistake, from every step taken in the wrong direction. The most important thing?

Know yourself. Recognise your own strengths and weaknesses. Accept what you can and can't do. Vital skills for any rider.

But this also means that in order to achieve your full potential, you'll need to be able to recognise when you're about to fall into the snare called self-sabotage.

So let's take a look at some of the most common self-sabotaging traps around.

1. Perfectionism or fear of failure

By its very definition, going out to compete means measuring yourself against other people. That can be very frightening, and presents a potential threat to a person's ego. Wanting to control the uncontrollable (like Juliette wanting to make sure she'll beat the competition) is in many ways a perfectly understandable – even though entirely unrealistic – reaction. By setting goals that are vague and can vary from day to day, such as 'I'll only go once he and I feel ready.' What does that really mean? By whose standards? Yours? The judges? And at what level? By setting yourself these kinds of goals you'll simply make sure that you're never ready to go and expose yourself (and your ego).

2. Inability to plan ahead

Agreed, we all lead busy lives. Sometimes it is difficult to plan ahead, because things happen that we didn't anticipate. But sometimes, the inability to plan ahead can be an effective way to self-sabotage. By continuously feeling overwhelmed by the demands on your time and by never making an effort to structure your life differently, you'll provide yourself with the perfect excuse to remain stuck in the status quo.

3. Blaming others/external circumstances

No one really enjoys admitting they've made a mistake. Because that would mean that you're not all that competent and autonomous after all. Still though, some people take this to extremes. They'll attribute their own failings, mistakes and shortcomings (which are all perfectly human) to others or their environment. It's the perfect excuse, too, seeing that you can't be held responsible for someone else's behaviour. So, your inability to achieve your goals isn't your fault. Seriously, it's not…

4. Unrealistic expectations

The world and everyone in it should always try and help you out!

Sound ridiculous? Yes, it does. Still, people who self-sabotage like to believe that this is the case. Having a skewed view of how the world should always work in your favour is another neat excuse for never having to face a situation that is potentially threatening. Unless everyone and everything is doing their utmost to support you, you can't possibly be expected to put yourself out there.

Right?

5. Inability to say 'no'

People love to be loved, liked, approved of (it comes back to the basic human need of relatedness). Saying no might jeopardise other people's positive opinions of us. It might even violate some kind of unwritten social contract that we should always put other people's needs before our own. The fact that it then prevents us from doing what we had hoped to do or achieve, well, to the self-saboteur, that's just another bonus.

Obviously though, as comforting as self-sabotaging behaviour may be in the short term, it's a sure-fire way to prevent you from achieving your ambitions.

But is it possible to break the habits of a lifetime? Yes. It is.

But you need to question yourself and your actions. You'll need to be critical, rather than making excuses for why you did the things you did. You'll need to be analytical, trying to find ever better solutions to the problems you face. And you'll need to be curious, never being satisfied with just one answer, always needing to find out more.

In short, you need to be self-reflective.

The psychology literature refers to the process of self-reflection as a form of enlightenment, whereby individuals use their own experiences to learn from, and improve their own professional performance. What is more, self-reflection is a conscious process of learning, rather than simply thinking back at past experiences. Its main aim, therefore, is the discovery of additional knowledge, by analysing, evaluating and developing new meaning.

It's all about the what, why and how of performance improvement. It's also the mantra of German Olympic eventer Andreas 'Dibo' Dibowski. To him, questioning everything is key. Preferably every day.

'You're not going to get any answers if you don't ask.' [50]

With more high-profile victories and placings to his name than most riders could ever dream of, it would seem that his approach is paying dividends.

Every day, he analyses strengths and weaknesses. Of himself and of his horses. He considers every detail, without losing sight of the ultimate goal.

And after that's done? Well, then he gets down to it and starts working on himself and his horses. To him, it's the biggest challenge there is, to continuously push your limits, outgrow yourself time and again.

But self-reflection can be more difficult than it sounds. One of the foremost researchers on the subject of reflective practice, professor emeritus Donald Schön[51], introduces the idea that people (riders) can reflect 'on-action', e.g. they'll critically analyse what has happened, once they're done. They can also reflect 'in-action', meaning they'll be busy analysing their behaviour while they're doing whatever it is they're doing.

If you give it a try, you'll soon realise that both approaches can be overwhelmingly complex, with a myriad of thoughts and emotions running riot in your head. Which one do you give precedent to? Which one is actually important? And how can you be sure that, even after careful

---

50   Wolframm, I. (2012), *Dreamteam Pferd und Reiter: Persönlichkeitsbestimmung im Reitsport,* Stuttgart, Müller Rüschlikon

51   Schön, D. A. (1984), *The Reflective Practitioner: How Professionals Think in Action*, Basic Books, Inc.

thought, you've managed to successfully avoid the trap of self-sabotage (after all, sabotaging yourself can be ever so easy!).

As a result, several researchers have attempted to develop guidelines to help sift through the myriad of sensations. The reflective cycle by Professor Graham Gibbs[52], formerly Director of the Oxford Learning Institute at the University of Oxford, involves six steps that help attain the most from any experience:

1. Call it by its name

What happened at the event in question? This could be a training session or a competition that didn't go as planned.

2. What did it do to you?

What were your immediate thoughts? Did they influence how you felt? (Probably!) What happened next? Did your thoughts and emotions influence how you dealt with your horse?

3. What does it mean to you?

Now it's time to take stock of the situation. Which were the positive, which the negative aspects you can take away from the experience? (And just before you argue otherwise, there's a positive to every situation. You might just have to search a little harder.)

4. How did it happen?

So why did things happen the way they did? Is it your training, your preparation, your riding on the day? Did your or your horse's physical or mental abilities have something to do with it?

---

52 Gibbs, G. (1988), 'Learning by Doing', A guide to teaching and learning methods, Further Education Unit, Oxford Polytechnic

5. Is there more to it?

What are your immediate conclusions? Are there things you're not clear on? Do you need to talk things through with your trainer or a (horsey) friend? Might you need to consult your vet, your farrier, or any source of information?

6. What's your plan?

Now that you've analysed the situation, you can develop a plan for the future. Do you need to change anything in relation to the training or management of your horse? Might you approach your own mental or physical fitness somewhat differently? Do you need to prepare yourself/ your horse differently in the run up to a training session/a competition.

Sounds very tiring? After all, you want to ride horses, not to solve a quantum physics problem?

According to British Grand Prix dressage rider Wayne Channon, that's almost the same.

'Riding horses is intellectually challenging. Every problem can be solved by analysis.' [53]

And he should know. In addition to being one of the UK's most prominent dressage riders, Wayne has set up and run numerous multi-million pound businesses.

Possibly the best example that there's no real age limit in horse sports, Wayne started riding properly when he was 34 – an age at which other athletes think about retiring! When his trainer at the time, Grand Prix rider Vicky Thompson, said that he could have been a very good rider, if he'd only started riding ten years earlier, it was just the kind of challenge Wayne found impossible to resist. It turned out that the same kind of character

53   Wolframm, I. (2012), *Dreamteam Pferd und Reiter: Persönlichkeitsbestimmung im Reitsport*, Stuttgart, Müller Rüschlikon

traits that helped him succeed in the business world allowed him to excel in dressage too:

'I'm a strategist. Everything I do, I try to analyse. I want to understand it completely.'

That's exactly how he trains his horses. He really gets to know them, and rides them in such a way that they find working at the highest level easy. And should he run into difficulties, he tackles them, just like everything else, systematically, analytically, reflectively.

First, he looks at a problem from all angles. He analyses and evaluates all the different elements. Then, after careful consideration, he develops the relevant strategy to solve them, one at a time.

That's what you need to do, too.

No excuses.

Just solutions.

PART II

MENTAL SKILLS
TO TRAIN YOUR MIND

CHAPTER 7

GOAL-SETTING: PLANNING YOUR JOURNEY

'I really dream of participating in the Olympic Games one day.'[54]
Athina Onassis

It's a sentiment recognised by thousands, if not millions, of riders. Competing at the Olympics. It's the biggest – the ultimate – dream. Athina Onassis de Miranda, sole surviving descendant to the Greek shipping magnate Aristotle Onassis, dares to say it out loud.

Chances are, at some point, she'll achieve it too. Make no mistake, when she does, it will have had very little to do with her wealth. While money can obviously help secure some of the 'trappings' any rider needs (a good horse, a good trainer, the right kind of facilities), the attributes needed to become outstanding, whether they're technical, physical or mental, she'll have to work on herself.

She's already got the one thing she needs to get her started. A dream.

And yet… even though all-important in the quest to achieve something great, at the beginning a dream is just that. A dream. Nothing more.

Until that dream is turned into a goal.

At first glance, the distinction might seem arbitrary, superfluous even. Surely, as long as it's there, in the rider's head, a dream is a goal and a goal is a dream?

It is undoubtedly true that having a dream is a definite plus. The attitudes essential to success, such as passion, determination and perseverance, can only be mustered if you are truly excited. And dreams do excite. They ignite the power within.

---

54   Mas, E. (2014), 'My Kingdom Mi Casa', *Horse Sport International*, Issue 2

But power needs direction, otherwise it'll simply evaporate. This is what goals have been invented for. A goal implies direction and, as a result, a path that leads toward it. A path made to walk on. Dreams turned into goals are fantasies about to be turned into reality.

Unfortunately – and here comes the 'but' you've undoubtedly been waiting for – the simple act of telling yourself that your deepest desire has now become your goal isn't going to make it happen. At least it's not very likely.

Why? Because most of the time (and allow me to stick with my original analogy here), the path is long.

Picture it, if you will...

There you are, at base camp in the Himalayas or some other impossibly high mountain range. The path ahead is narrow. Still, at least it starts off with only a gentle incline. Snaking back and forth through a range of trees, you catch yourself thinking the start of the journey looks easy enough. The trees provide plenty of shelter from the elements and a liberal sprinkling of pine needles make the ground soft and springy to walk on. Finally, you're going to follow your dreams. You feel great. Alert. Energised. Looking forward to your journey. So off you go.

After a while, your surroundings change. Soft, mossy ground turns to rubble (remember, you're in a mountainous region!). Sometimes a pebble will lodge itself in your shoe, sometimes you'll trip up over stones as big as bowling balls. And sometimes rocks the size of baby elephants will force you to either change course or climb over them.

All you want to do is sit down. You're so tired... Yet you struggle on.

But if you think the worst is over, think again. Where there was stone, there's now ice and snow. The rock face has become incredibly steep. Your feet find little purchase, and you're sliding all over the place, sometimes even back down the mountain. The path has entirely disappeared by now, and all you can see is some mountain top somewhere up in the distance, half-hidden by cloud cover.

Finally, you do sit down (if you've even lasted this long). Once you've sat down though, you might decide it's much too comfortable and you don't want to get up anymore. Suddenly you find that you crave all the things you've had to go without for a very long time. Hunger and thirst have become almost unbearable. And I'm not talking about food or drink either. Having a 'life'. Going shopping or to the cinema. Reading a book. Partying with friends. Spending more time with family.

Suddenly, you start to wonder whether any of it is worth the effort…

You tell yourself that if it's that hard, your dream might not be worth pursuing after all. This is where the principle of goal-setting comes in. One big goal, also often referred to as a 'long-term goal' is fantastic to start planning your journey, but once you've got that, you need to make sure you've got pit-stops on the way to refuel, and if necessary, readjust.

Athina Onassis de Miranda, who has fought her way up the show jumping tree with incredible determination, guts and a refusal to give in, proves she knows all about planning her journey. Right after she'd confessed to her dreams, she goes on to say the following:

> *'But we'll see, one year at a time. There's still a lot of work to do. First, I'm going to try to be ready for this summer's World Equestrian Games.'* [55] (Note: Athina referred to the 2014 World Equestrian Games in Normandy, France, where she represented Greece.)

Athina talks about nothing more and nothing less than medium-term and short-term goals. In order to reach her ultimate goal, her dream of competing at the Olympics, she uses a number of stepping stones to get there, the World Equestrian Games 2014 being one of them. But she also alludes to other goals, merely by stating that there's 'still a lot of work to do'. Considering how far she's already come, she'll know precisely what 'a lot of work' entails.

Put simply (because, really, it is simple) in order to reach a long-term goal, you'll need medium-term goals as milestones to guide and facilitate your journey. Reaching them allows you to admire how far you've come already (giving you an immediate confidence boost), and to realise that the top of the mountain – your ultimate goal – has just moved that bit closer.

---

55   Mas, E. (2014), 'My Kingdom Mi Casa', *Horse Sport International*, Issue 2

In horsey terms these include a qualifying show or moving up a level.

Short-term goals are, both literally and figuratively, the steps you need to take to reach your medium-term goals. They might include anything from getting the right equipment, learning a new skill (whether physical, technical or mental), to buying another horse or finding another trainer.

But before we discuss how to discover exactly what you might need to get to where you want to go, let's take a look at some underlying principles of how to set the most effective – and thus most satisfying – kind of goals, regardless of whether they're long-, medium-, or short-term.

SMART-LY DOES IT

For starters, there's SMART. In all likelihood, you will have heard of it, perhaps at school or in some other, business-related setting[56] . The acronym stands for Specific, Measurable, Achievable, Relevant and Timebound, and outlines basic yet essential goal characteristics that have been shown to improve your chance of actually reaching your goal. So here's how to run your own goals through your very own SMART check:

S = Specific

Are your goals clear and unambiguous? Do you know what, why, who, where? There should be no room for vagaries otherwise it becomes very, very hard to stick to the path!

M = Measurable

How long, how much, how many – are you able to tell when you've achieved your goal? If you can't, you could end up like the proverbial dog chasing its tail.

---

56   Principles of effective goal-setting were originally investigated and defined in a business environment

A = Achievable

Is your goal realistic? Will you actually be able to get there at some point, or is there something that definitely, absolutely prevents you from ever achieving it? (For example wanting to compete in a Young Rider's competition even though you're 30 years old. Or hoping to join the national team in show jumping, even though your horse cannot jump to save its life.)

R = Relevant

This one is really simple. Does your goal matter to you? If it doesn't, you won't care enough to make it happen. This is why the dream should always come first.

T = Timebound

Set yourself a deadline – by when do you want to have achieved your goal?

So then, next time you're off on another big adventure, you should always, *always* run your goals through a SMART check!

Sounds simple enough, right? But there's more…

THE 'BIG FIVE' OF GOAL-SETTING

The fathers of goal-setting, Dr Edwin Locke, Dean's Professor (Emeritus) of Leadership and Motivation at the R.H. Smith School of Business at the University of Maryland, and Dr Gary Latham, Secretary of State Professor of Organisational Effectiveness and Professor of Organisational Behaviour and HR Management at Rotman School of Management), spent decades researching the most effective way to set goals in a business context.[57] Since then, their ideas and theories have been applied effectively to performance

---

57 In 1990, they published their seminal work, 'A Theory of Goal Setting and Task Performance'

in sports. In addition to SMART, Locke and Latham developed five additional principles that considerably improve our chances of reaching our goals and our dreams.

1. Clarity

Goals must be clear. It's obvious. If you don't know where you're headed or are unable to recognise it once you've got there, you're unlikely to get very far (and if, by chance, you do, you're unlikely to reproduce it a second time). The most obvious and poignant example is going to a show and setting yourself the goal to 'do your best'. While laudable in and of itself, it's not very clear at all. What is your best? How much effort does it entail? How would you go about repeating it? Especially if you're intent on producing sustainable performances, you need to know whether you're hoping to complete a 100 km endurance ride in under 13 hours or whether 14 hours will do. You need to be clear whether you are aiming for a dressage score of 60 or 70 per cent. You'll have to make up your mind whether you're happy with slightly oval circles in a reining class or whether you want them to be perfectly round. Perhaps even more importantly, you'll need to be sure whether and when you've achieved your goal. Knowing that you've achieved what you've set out to do will be like a pat on the back. It'll do wonders for your confidence and give you the boost that'll sustain you for the next part of your journey.

The good thing?

If you've run your goals through the SMART check, chances are you're already pretty clear to where you're headed.

2. Challenge

Drs Locke and Latham are adamant in their research about this: challenging (yet realistic) goals produce the best effects. Why? Because by setting yourself a challenge you are moving outside of your own comfort zone. You are essentially forcing yourself to improve one or more aspects of yourself, as otherwise you'll be unlikely to cope with the new situation. But once you've managed to acquire whatever you needed, you'll see your performance improve, too. Say you've challenged yourself to compete at a higher class in show jumping (assuming that you've got a horse that has the scope). Fences are higher, distances trickier. You'll need to be more accurate, have more control. So you work on acquiring the necessary skills. Suddenly your horse listens much better, is softer in the mouth, more reactive to the leg. What used to be a challenge suddenly turns into something you can quite easily do. Another pat on the back. Another boost for your journey.

3. Commitment

This is where we return to our analogy of the treacherous mountain path. To keep going even when the road turns rocky, slippery or impossible to see requires considerable commitment. To be truly committed, you need to believe in your ultimate goal. It needs to be intrinsically yours, and yours only. It shouldn't – mustn't – be driven or directed by any extrinsic, external forces (for example what other people might wish you to do, the lure of money or fame, that sort of thing). In essence, it all comes back to being able to control your own life. We've already discussed the importance of self-concept, i.e. knowing and understanding the essence that is you. Any goals in line with your own self-concept will foster much more commitment than if someone else had told you what to do. Which, incidentally, tallies with the notion that human beings are intrinsically motivated to be autonomous. Take Athina. In all likelihood, she could have been anybody, done anything. But she didn't want to be just anybody, do just anything. She wanted to be a rider. So at 17 she moved to Belgium to train with show jumping legend Nelson Pessoa – where she also met her future husband, Brazilian show jumper 'Doda' Alvaro de Miranda Neto. Her father was dead set against the match. So, to get her own way, Athina launched a legal battle against him. And won. It says a lot about the young Greek's level of commitment to her goals.

4. Feedback

Obviously, feedback at its most objective is vital to check whether you're on track, whether you have already achieved your goal. That's why goal clarity is such a vital element. Without clarity, no possibility for objective feedback. Without objective feedback little chance of knowing where you stand.

But this isn't all. Feedback can be so much more… As we've discussed on numerous occasions – no rider is an island. Interaction with others is important, if not vital, to sustain motivation, to provide a different perspective, a helping hand, whatever is required at any given moment. Such interaction with others is equally important when it comes to trying to achieve your goals. Receiving feedback allows you to connect with the world around you. It is a testament to your innate desire for relatedness. Sometimes, the right comment at the right time can be the difference between tackling that one big oxer or deciding you don't have the guts to do it after all. This does entail of course that you surround yourself with the kind of people that are able to give you the right kind of feedback at the right time – another good reason to keep working away at your network!

5. Complexity

Now we get to the very tricky part – especially when it comes to the ambitious individual. In order for your goals to lead to ultimate success, they must strike the right balance between challenging and achievable. The most obvious mistake to make, which also happens to be incredibly difficult to avoid, is that of making your goal(s) too complex. It's a sure-fire way of over asking yourself, and, as a result, overexerting yourself. Wanting to achieve too much too soon is as bad as setting goals that are too easy. In order to keep your motivation, performance and enjoyment at an even keel, you need to pace yourself. In practical (yet slightly exaggerated) terms, this might mean don't attempt to teach your horse piaffe and passage if what you really want to do is jump a round of show jumps (unless of course, working on piaffe and passage is the only way to get him to collect). If you've got a whole yard full of horses to ride, don't attempt to groom them all to world class standard.

Make choices.

Prioritise.

Dare to say no.

PERFORMANCE PROFILING –
MICRO-MANAGING YOUR GOALS

But even once you're relatively clear about your goals and you've ticked them off against the goal-setting criteria by Latham and Locke, there's still more work to be done. Now it's time to take a realistic look at yourself and the immediate environment you operate in. Which aspects might need improving in order for you to actually reach all of your ambitions, which ones are already well established? In sport psychology circles such a technique is called performance profiling, but it might just as well be called micro-managing your goals…

As the name might suggest, it helps athletes (riders) to develop a realistic profile of themselves and what they've got to work on to reach the kind of performance they desire.

This is how it works: think of all the elements a rider at the very top of his or her game might need. Anything ranging from riding skills, to physical fitness, from horse power to management, from mental attitudes to mental skills. On a scale from 0 (not important at all) to 10 (can't do without), grade each of those elements according to its importance to top-level performance. Some elements might be worth a 10, some only a 7 or an 8. But it doesn't stop here. Now you need to grade yourself (again, on a scale from 0 to 10). Try to be as honest as you possibly can. Don't exaggerate your skills, simply because you'd like to be better than you are, but don't be overly modest either. The point of this exercise is to pin-point which areas you need to work on in order to improve – which you can only do to full effect if you've created as objective a profile of yourself as possible. At the end, detract your own score from the top rider's score. You'll end up with a list of scores that will demonstrate all too clearly your personal strong points as well as where there's room for improvement.

To help you on your way, I've included a short example performance profile. You might decide you'll need additional categories or that some of the ones I've included don't apply to your particular situation. That's all good. After all, this is going to be your performance profiling exercise, so you need to agree with it and feel autonomous while doing it. As we know, being in control is the safest way of creating commitment!

CHARACTERISTICS	TOP RIDER SCORE OVERALL IMPORTANCE (1 – 10)	YOUR SCORE 1 – 10	DISCREPANCY
RIDING RELATED			
Ability to keep rhythm			
Seeing distances			
Working the horse round an outline			
Training horses to be 'On the aids'			
Developing feel for the horse			
PHYSICAL			
Balance			
Co-ordination			
Aerobic Fitness			
Strength			
Quality of sleep			
MENTAL SKILLS			
Commitment			
Staying calm under pressure			
Rising to the challenge			
Tackling problems head on			

CHARACTERISTICS	TOP RIDER SCORE OVERALL IMPORTANCE (1 – 10)	YOUR SCORE 1 – 10	DISCREPANCY
Handling setbacks well			
Getting on with things following a mistake			
Maintaining a positive outlook			
Keeping your focus			
Believing in yourself			
Focusing on self-improvement			
Self-reflection			
MANAGEMENT			
Stabling that guarantees horses' safety and welfare			
Arena			
Other training facilities			
Trusted team (e.g. grooms, vets, farrier, saddler, physio, etc.)			
Secure finances			

Once you're done, you'll have a solid draft of the road map for your journey with lots and lots of short- or medium-term goals (depending on which element we're talking about) that'll serve as stepping stones. As you tackle them, each one in turn, make sure you stick to the goal-setting principles discussed at the beginning of the chapter. Keep it SMART and in line with the 'Big Five', and you'll be amazed how quickly your own performance will soar.

And just before you say it... Yes, there's some work involved in tackling goal-setting effectively. But as they say – a little effort now will go a long way in and towards the future.

HOW TO SET YOURSELF UP TO SUCCEED

So that's the bigger picture of your life as a rider planned, organised and mapped out. But what about the kind of goals you might wish to set for a show? First off, the same principles apply. Be SMART about them. Make them clear and challenging. Ensure commitment. Organise opportunities for feedback. Keep them simple.

But despite the relative simplicity of these rules, in the heat of the moment, e.g. when it's 'show-time', riders tend to forget the things they so carefully worked out. Suddenly they end up formulating goals that might not only be counterproductive but downright dangerous...

We've already discussed the importance of defining your own level of success, and the importance of putting the 'task' ahead of your 'ego'. Still, the topic is of such importance to both satisfaction and success that it is worth looking at one more time and from a slightly different angle.

When we talk about goal-setting for competition, we tend to focus on three separate goal categories: outcome goals, performance goals and process goals.

Outcome goals quite simply refer to the – you guessed it – competitive outcome. They are comparative in nature and as such focus only on winning, being placed, being last, and as such exist pretty much independently of actual performances. In simple terms, this means you can achieve an outcome goal of winning a class even though you performed poorly by the simple expedient that all the other competitors performed worse than you did.

Unless Lady Luck is your fairy godmother and by way of personal favour grants you a win at every class you enter, outcome goals are notoriously difficult to control as they depend on so many external factors (and most importantly, other riders). This is why outcome goals can cause considerable anxiety. The moment you don't know what a situation demands from you, your thought-processes will go into overdrive, frantically trying to figure out what to do and how to do it – without ever achieving a satisfactory answer. Suddenly, instead of focusing on the job in hand, your brain is otherwise engaged, worrying more about the rider warming up next to you than on what you're supposed to be doing.

Performance goals on the other hand help you focus on just yourself and your horse. They generally are measured as objectively as possible and thus provide a yardstick with which to measure your own performance – independent of what other competitors are up to. Achieving a clear cross-country round with no time penalties, a 70 per cent dressage or vaulting score has absolutely nothing to do with any other competitor (or at least, it shouldn't), but only depends on how you performed on the day.

Remember Adelinde Cornelissen's quote? In preparation for the 2012 Dressage World Cup Final she said:

> *'Most importantly, I ride for myself. I ride because I enjoy it so much and because I love performing together with my equine partner. Winning really isn't important. In fact, I use competition as a marker to see how far I have come in my training.'* [58]

Aiming for a personal best rather than outshining the rest enables you to control the things that are in fact controllable. Still, the biggest pitfall here is simply to go with your performance goal without having any plan as to how to achieve it.

This is where process goals come in. Let's take your goal-setting for competition yet another step further and think of exactly what you need to do. Be specific. Be technical. Talk aids, hands, legs, seat. How do you need to ride your horse? Go beyond the 'he needs to work through from behind'. Think how you are going to get him working through from behind. Don't stop at 'he needs to respond to my leg throughout the test', but specify what you're going to do to make sure that he does. The more specific you

58   Wolframm, I. (2012), 'Mind over Matter: How mental training can raise your game', *Horse Sport International*, Issue 2

are, the more in control you'll feel and the more confident you'll be that you can achieve what you've set out to do.

Having said all of this, there remain some 'real life' issues that require addressing.

Even though focusing on your own performance rather than competitive outcome will lead to more consistent performances, there might come a time when you'll have to take a sneaky peak at what your competitors are doing. After all, going out to compete means wanting to do well – the dangers of comparison be damned. That means that once in a while you'll need to check that your own goals are still in sync with reality. If, for example, your aim is to make the team of one of the leading dressage nations, and you're aiming for a 65 per cent Grand Prix, you'll need to think again – and add at least another 10 per cent to your performance score.

TROUBLE-SHOOTING...

Which brings us neatly to our last, and very short, point…

Goals are great. They really work. Set goals that are right for you and your situation, and they'll see you through to the end.

But now and again you might have to deal with a diversion along the way. Why? Because life is tricky and so are horses. This means that from time to time, your situation might change and you'll have to cope. You might have to tweak your goals, readjust them here or there. You might have to postpone achieving them or replace one with another. But as long as you do them within the broader framework you've set yourself, you'll still be able to get there in the end.

Remember Margie Goldstein-Engle and the spell of accidents and injuries that plagued her career in the 1990s? No doubt she would have had to readjust her short-term and sometimes even her medium-term goals. In the end though, she still got there. Virtually unbeaten for a decade.

Sometimes you might even have to change your goals half-way through a competition. In fact, as Mary King demonstrates, approaching your goals flexibly can be an important strategy:

'I would walk the course, I would make up my mind how I was riding fences, but then I would also have my options open. If say, later on in the day, I am watching riders and certain things aren't working quite as how I thought they were going to work, such as distances or lines. I would maybe change my gears. It is quite often that it's your gut instinct that would tell you how you would ride those fences.'

So you see, setting your goals is essential to success. But being able to stay flexible, and revise those goals as and when the situation requires, is equally as important.

At the end of the day, it's all part of what we call competitive sport.

CHAPTER 8

MANAGING STRESS: STAYING CALM AND CARRYING ON

Every year, the Reem Acra World Cup Dressage Final is one of the highlights on the competitive calendar. For an entire season, the world's most accomplished dressage riders battle it out for points, only to come together at the end for one final showdown. Winning the World Cup Title – it's something that only the best in the sport can pull off.

Adelinde Cornelissen, Dutch English teacher-cum-dressage rider is, without a shadow of doubt, one of the best. Since the year 2009, she and her partner, chestnut gelding Jerich Parzival, have been collecting one prestigious title after another, including, in 2011, the World Cup title. One year later, in 2012, an Olympic year no less, she was expected to defend her title. All eyes were on her, gauging her form, judging her, speculating on things to come.

To say 'the pressure was on' would be an understatement. As far as Adelinde is concerned, that's just fine…

> *'The more expectations there are, the better I feel about the whole thing. I need that pressure to be able to perform to the very best of my ability.'* [59]

Adelinde said she needed pressure?

Well, she got it.

After a somewhat lacklustre Grand Prix, the German horse–rider combo of Helen Langehanenberg and Damon Hill was breathing right down her neck. In order to clinch the title in the Freestyle, Adelinde needed

---

[59] Wolframm, I. (2012) 'Mind over Matter: How mental training can raise your game', *Horse Sport International*, Issue 2

to pull something spectacular out of the hat. And she did – winning the 2012 Reem Acra World Cup title with just one point ahead of Helen.

Impressive? Absolutely.

Easy to emulate? A little more difficult…

Unfortunately, not all of us have the mental grit to use pressure to our advantage.

Picture the following scenario and ask yourself whether any of it rings a bell.

Roberta Jacobs is a talented rider. She's in her early twenties, but, really, she could be any age. (By the way, Roberta could also be Robert, but – whether we like it or not – women tend to suffer more from the following problem.)

Two years ago, Roberta bought a promising four-year old with outstanding bloodlines. At least, that was the breeder's explanation for the nausea-inducing price tag. So far, the breeder's prediction seems to be spot on. The horse, let's call him 'Good Enough', short for 'So You Think You're Good Enough To Be Riding Me', has been doing well in training. He's obedient to the leg, forward going, with a lot of movement. Roberta's trainer keeps telling her, 'if you don't mess him up, Good Enough can go all the way.' Obviously, Roberta is determined not to mess him up. But she's really worried that she might. In fact, she worries about most things. Whether Good Enough will stay sound. Whether he's got the right rug on. Whether her bandages match her saddlecloth. What makes it even worse is that she's convinced that most of the people at the yard are waiting for her to slip up. She thinks she can see it in their eyes; they think that a horse like that is just too good for her.

Today Roberta and Good Enough will be competing in their first show together. They've practised at home and their trainer thinks they're ready. Roberta is determined to show everyone that she's the right kind of rider for Good Enough. Yesterday, she spent ages washing, grooming and plaiting Good Enough, just to make sure he's as pretty as he can be. You can imagine her distress when, as she enters Good Enough's stable, she finds him covered in manure and stray hairs sticking out of his plaits like hedgehog spines. He must have had a good roll during the night. Unfortunately, Roberta only has half an hour before the horse lorry gets here. Starting to panic, she decides to give Good Enough a quick wash with the hose.

Perhaps it was the way she threw on his head collar, or perhaps Good Enough simply didn't like being shouted at because he wouldn't move over in the stable. Whatever the reason, Good Enough decides that the washing area is scary. He's now refusing to even go near it and, after fifteen minutes of fighting a losing battle, Roberta has to make do with quickly brushing him off. The plaits will have to stay the way they are now, because – oh hell! – the lorry's already here. Roberta's trainer instructs her to get all of Good Enough's stuff, while he loads the horse. Good Enough follows the trainer like a little lamb.

On the way to the show the lorry is held up for a good twenty minutes, as some overzealous workmen decided to rip open the road at 8 am on a Sunday. But there's still enough time, or so Roberta's trainer keeps reassuring Roberta. She doesn't believe him. By now, she's sitting right at the edge of her seat, her breath coming out in short, sharp bursts.

Finally, they get to the show. It's a busy show. There are flags and tents and what seems like a million people. What is worse, they're all clustered in small groups around the warm-up and the main ring, commenting on everyone and everything. There are a couple of riders already warming up. Roberta can't help but compare herself and Good Enough to them. It doesn't look good. She tries to swallow down her rising panic, but all the water in her mouth has gone to her palms.

No time to think about sweaty hands or dry mouths, as Roberta's trainer has just come back from the secretary's office to tell her that the starting time has changed. She needs to get on Good Enough now. Right now!

Getting to the warm-up comes close to Roberta's personal idea of hell. Good Enough spooks, baulks, then leaps forward, only to spook again. Her shoulders and the top of her arms feel like they're on fire from holding on to the reins. When they finally get to the warm-up, Roberta's knackered. But at least she doesn't have to worry about inadvertently flattening innocent spectators.

Warming up goes 'okay', not terribly well, but not terribly, either. Good Enough is neither as through nor as responsive to the leg as he is at home, but at least he has stopped jumping around. Roberta worries that if she asks too much, she'll upset him, so she sticks to riding a few circles and transitions. Time's up anyway.

Ding, ding, ding. There goes the bell. Now she's going to show them all. Only winning will do… Guess what. Roberta didn't show anybody anything. She didn't win either. Instead, she went home thinking that she should try to find another sport.

Any of this sound familiar? If it does, you're in good company. Many, if not most, riders get stressed, become anxious, start to panic at some point or other and usually when it matters most. There are many reasons for it and we'll discuss them all in turn a little later on.

In Roberta's case, she tried to live up to an image she thought others had of her. Secretly, she was worried that, perhaps, she's not good enough for Good Enough. Other people's comments about the quality of her horse only made things worse. Roberta got stressed because things didn't turn out the way she had planned. She hadn't counted on things going wrong and when they did, she didn't know how to cope. She was left feeling out of control. Having no control can be very scary. It stresses people. It stressed Roberta. Stress on top of stress leads to, exactly, stress…

And unless you know how to deal with it, it can put a real dampener on your performance.

First things first though. Let's take a look at what this thing called stress or anxiety or nerves or butterflies in your tummy actually is.

There are some people who suffer from it more often. It's literally in their nature. They break out in a cold sweat when confronted with situations that might leave other people cold. In sport psychological circles this is called trait anxiety. It is a semi-permanent feature of an individual's personality, rather than something that only happens once in a while. Our imaginary rider, Roberta, is just such an individual. You probably spotted it already. She worries about all sorts of things, including Good Enough's health and the colour of his bandages. People might dismiss quite a few of her concerns as silly (admittedly, some of them are), but this is just part of being 'highly strung'. The personal radar that goes off whenever there's the potential for things to go wrong is simply more developed. By the way, if you think you might be more trait anxious than average, don't despair! Even though you are unlikely to ever stop worrying completely (nor should you want to, because it can be a useful trait to have), you *can* learn to effectively manage your own level of anxiety.

But even if you consider yourself a very cool customer, once in a while, you might experience situations that completely freak you out. This is called 'state' anxiety and suggests that the condition is temporary – and might last from several minutes to several days. Going out to compete, especially if you're going for the first time, is just such a situation and likely to set you on edge. Once again though, even though uncomfortable, these nerves can be useful. The key is simply to learn how to deal with them.

We also differentiate between cognitive and somatic anxiety. Cognitive anxiety happens purely in your mind. Worries, doubts, uncertainties and insecurities run riot in your head in times of stress or pressure. The thought of messing up a horse for example. Or performing below expectations. Or not being liked by judges. Or disappointing a trainer.

Somatic anxiety describes the immediate physical reaction to anxiety, and the resulting strain on the body can be considerable. When people get stressed (or anxious, or worried), they breathe more quickly. Their breaths become shallow and rise to their chests. Their heart rates will increase too, and their muscles will start to contract. From an evolutionary point of view, all these physical changes make perfect sense. When confronted with a 'stressor', e.g. a threat to life or limb, such as a mountain lion mistaking you for his lunch, the body readies itself for a 'fight or flight' reaction. More frequent breaths mean more oxygen to be taken up by the red blood cells, which then have nothing better to do than deliver it directly to the muscles. Once there, oxygen combined with glucose is transformed into Adenosine Triphosphate (ATP), the energy currency of the body. Add a liberal dose of the body's own legal drug adrenaline (it gives you wings) and cortisol (helps with the wing-giving, among other things), and the body is ready for whatever it takes to stay alive. The thing is, the body doesn't differentiate all that well between what constitutes a real threat (a mountain lion, a car freewheeling towards you, a burglar caught mid-heist) and what is primarily perceived. In the grand scheme of things, losing a competition isn't really the end of the world, but in the heat of the moment, that's what it feels like. So the body reacts. Why?

It tries to protect your ego! A threat to the 'ego', e.g. to your own identity, can feel as severe and dangerous as the thought of falling off and breaking your leg. Especially to those individuals whose identity hinges on winning or not losing (ego-orientation – see chapter 2), the potential for performing poorly can cause an advanced stress reaction.

So regardless of whether stress is real (a physical threat) or perceived (a threat to the ego), whether it's really 'out there' or just in the rider's head, the body will react the same. As a result, the rider will feel out of control, both physically and mentally. Not being in control isn't a lot of fun though, and especially in horse sports, losing control can be detrimental.

The reason? Horses are highly sensitive flight animals. They'll react first and ask questions, well, never… What's more, horses are trained using principles of learning theory. After many, many repetitions, they'll finally learn to associate a certain cue (an 'aid') with a movement[60]. Put your leg on and apply a certain amount of pressure and your horse (should) move forward. Move your leg slightly further back, and, again, use just the right amount of pressure, and your horse will respond with a few steps sideways. Then, close your hand softly around your reins, sit up tall, and your horse will slow down. Now picture Roberta. She's sick with nerves. Her heart's racing, her palms are sweaty, her breathing is short, sharp and shallow, her muscles feel as hard as iron. She's supposed to be giving very subtle aids. A touch of the leg here, a whisper of a half-halt there. It's not going to happen, is it? Can you seriously blame Good Enough for behaving differently at a show? Of course not. Roberta was behaving differently too. But because she was so caught up in being worried about all the things going on around, and wondering whether she herself was good enough, she simply didn't realise it.

And yet – those physical reactions to a stressor,[61] *the arousal of the body, don't have to be a problem.*

---

60 There are people much more qualified to talk about this subject than I am. I suggest you read their work too, if you're interested. In my view, one of the top books on the subject is McGreevy and McLean's book *Equitation Science*, Wiley, (2010)

61 Sport psychology researchers like to use the term because it implies neutrality, as opposed to anxiety (which has negative connotations) or excitement (a positive interpretation). 'Arousal' implies simply that the body is reacting physically but there are no negative or positive associations attached to it

Adrenalin is the body's very own energy drink. It energises people, boosting reaction times and the ability to concentrate. Faster breathing rates and a pumping heart mean more oxygen, while cortisol floods the body with glucose. The result? More fuel for working muscles. More time before fatigue hits. Greater levels of concentration (don't forget, concentration also uses up quite a bit of glucose!). So you see, stress can be a very good thing. It can help improve performance.

A MATTER OF INTERPRETATION

The key is how you interpret the entire experience. Instead of viewing stress as something that undermines your performance, try and turn it on its head. See it as a sensation that makes sense, and therefore is helpful. One that makes you more alert, more focused, and generally better able to deal with the challenges facing you.

Nick Burton is adamant that anxiety is part of the game, but that the key is to treat it as something useful. And he should know. As an active competitor, he rode at four-star level in eventing and national level Grand Prix dressage. These days, he's a list one Grand Prix dressage judge, a World Class Development Programme dressage coach, and he officiated at the 2012 London Olympic Games, the 2011 Eventing Senior European Championships in Luhmühlen, and many other high profile events. When I asked him whether he could describe his own experience, this is what he had to say:

'I think if you wanted to describe anxiety that's part of the nerves that are part of the preparation. And that is something that I want to take place, otherwise it really doesn't matter anymore and I am not prepared because if you don't get a little bit of nerves, a little bit of jitters and a little bit of butterflies then you're not really preparing yourself to compete. If you're just riding, or running or walking, or whatever it is – you're not going to compete, and trying to do your best. So that's a very important part of it. And to deal with it is to actually use that as part of my focus rather than to say "oh, I feel nervous, that's

97

going to debilitate my performance", is to say "now I feel like I'm competing". And not just riding at home. I'm competing, this is part of it, I feel nervous. I know that if I am feeling like that I am ready to compete, I am ready to do my best. If I go and I'm not interested, I'm not focused, I'm not nervous, I am not acting in a way that makes me perform well, then I would be more concerned about not feeling anxiety than feeling anxiety. So I expect it and I want it. So that I know that I am ready.'

And in the unlikely event you still don't believe it – what, in terms of physical sensation at least, is the difference between anxiety and excitement? There isn't one. Not really. It's merely the perception that differs (it's also called direction of arousal). Excitement is generally considered as something positive while most of us view anxiety as something negative – even though the physical symptoms are pretty much the same.

Interesting? You bet! Because the most important part to dealing with arousal, be it anxiety, be it excitement, is that you learn to interpret it as something that is useful. Something that'll help you perform rather than make you fail.

Many athletes actually enjoy the feeling of anxiety. In their eyes, it helps to keep them sharp, on the lookout, ready for anything. It makes them try just that little bit harder. Others might prefer to label their anxiety differently. They might want to go with excitement and prefer to see it as a positive rush.

So how do you transform anxiety into an emotion that's helpful? How do you learn to interpret those butterflies in your stomach as a signal that says 'ready', rather than 'ready to run away and hide'? How do you turn 'scary' into 'challenge'?

Let's start with a general concept before we turn to some more practical tips further on. We generally get stressed whenever:

1. We're not sure if we've got the required skills
2. We're not sure whether we're able to meet expectations
3. We consider the outcome important in some way.

Those are very powerful conditions and, if managed incorrectly, can freak out the most relaxed individual. So let's have a look at how you might go about restructuring the competitive experience in order to interpret those competitive jitters of yours in a positive light.

1. Do you think you've got what it takes?

This one is all about how you perceive your own level of skill compared to the requirements of the situation. Note the word 'perceived' here. Even though it is of course rather important that you are actually able to ride at a certain level, it's even more important that you believe yourself capable. In fact, this was one of Roberta's problems. She worried she might not do a good enough job with Good Enough. Yet her trainer thought she was, in fact, good enough, providing sufficient indication that the problem was imagined rather than real. So if you are unsure whether you actually have the necessary skills you need, try writing them down. Compose a list of all the various requirements of a competition (or any situation you are concerned about). Write down what you can and can't do. Think of previous competitions, but also training sessions. Can you tick off all, or most of the boxes? Yes? That's a pretty good indication that you do have the necessary skill to go off and compete. High time, therefore, to view the situation you're facing as a challenge. A challenge you might even consider looking forward to...

2. Whose expectations are we talking about?

Ask yourself (honestly!) who you might be trying to impress. Yourself? Or someone else? I'd like to take you back to the concept of ego- or task-orientation (see chapter 2). If you make it your main mission in life to persuade the rest of the world to like you, to think you're the most wonderful rider, to beat every other rider all of the time in competition, you're putting yourself in an impossible situation. One that is, quite simply, impossible to control. You have no influence over what others might think or do, how they might behave or act in any given situation. This lack of control will leave you fretting virtually all of the time, because, deep down you'll know you can't control the situation, yet you'll continue to try.

This is what Roberta did. She desperately wanted everyone to think she was a good rider. She worried what people at the show might think, she worried about other competitors. But not for one moment did she think of what she had to do to give Good Enough the best possible experience. So in order to avoid feeling out of control and at the mercy of others, focus on what you expect from yourself instead. Set yourself goals you can control (see chapter 7). Focus on your own performance and how to get there. It's your show. Enjoy it.

3.   What it all means to you

If you are a competitive rider, a show matters. Of course it does. If it didn't matter, why would you bother. Still, sometimes it can be useful to keep things in perspective. One show is just that. One show. By attaching too much importance to one particular event, you will end up putting yourself under unnecessary pressure. Nayel Nassar agrees. In his early twenties, he's already the highest ranked Egyptian show jumping rider, with two World Cup Finals under his belt. When asked how he copes with the pressure of performing for his country, he says:

'Personally, I like pressure as a rider but the key is to treat each round like the last.' [62]

So whenever you start to feel overwhelmed by the pressure of one particular event, try putting it in perspective. Even if you're about to compete at the Olympics, the things you'll have to do in the ring shouldn't be any different to what you've been doing for years – at home, at any other show. At the end of the day, all you'll need to do is ride. There's really nothing more to it. So then, those nerves are just your body's way of telling you that you're ready. So go and do your thing…

62   Miller, K. (2013), 'Young Guns: Nayel Nassar', *Horse Sport International*, Issue 2

YOUR PERFECT ZONE

So once you begin to realise that the butterflies in your tummy are actually quite useful (a little bit like the judge's bell, telling you it's your turn), you should try and figure out how many of them you actually need in order to be at your absolute best.

For a very long time, people thought all athletes performed best with just a modicum of arousal. Then, sport psychologist Yuri Hanin, Emeritus Professor at the Research Institute for Olympic Sports in Finland, turned up on the scene and taught everyone differently. In his theory entitled Individual Zones of Optimal Functioning (IZOF)[63], he argued that athletes differ in how much arousal they need to perform at their best. Some athletes need high levels of arousal, others need hardly any at all, and others still benefit from just the average amount. Riders are exactly the same. Some thrive on a little more 'oomph', while others do best when they're completely chilled. It's those tiny yet important differences that make life fun, so don't worry if your own level of 'oomph' is not the same as that of your best friend.

Rider 1	Good	Poor	Good
Rider 2	Poor	Good	Poor
Rider 3	Poor	Poor	Good
	Arousal level (on a scale from 0 – 10)		

Performing well in equine sports is, of course, not just about you. It's about the interaction between yourself and your horse. So just to make matters a little more complicated, consider this: if you ride several horses, optimal arousal levels may vary from one horse to the other. Perhaps you

---

63 Hanin, Y. L. (1997), 'Emotions and athletic performance: Individual zones of optimal functioning model', *European Yearbook of Sport Psychology*, pp. 1, 29-72

even compete in different disciplines, either with different horses, or with the same (such as in eventing). So it's your task to figure out how much arousal you need to perform at your best. Here's how.

YOUR 'OOMPH' SCALE

Think back to a time when you and your horse performed really well. If you've been struggling to perform in competition, think of a training session that went particularly well. On a scale from 0 to 10 (0 = dead as a dodo; 10 = ready to explode) how much arousal, e.g. how much 'oomph', did you feel? Then think of a time when things weren't going so well. Again, rate yourself on that 'oomph' scale and plot arousal vs. performance on a graph like the one below. Bear in mind though that the one below is just an example. Yours might end up looking very different. In all likelihood, there'll be a clear indication that you, too, have a Zone of Optimal Functioning. You might want to think of a few more examples to get as clear a picture as possible. And if you ride several horses, or compete in different disciplines, you might even consider drawing up one per horse/per discipline.

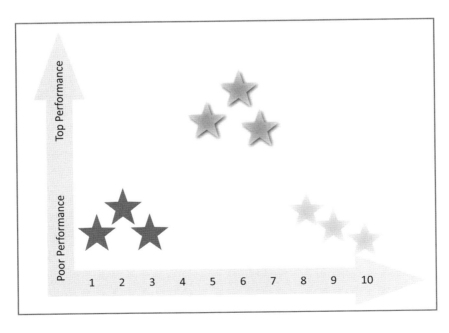

As you become more comfortable and confident with determining your own levels of optimal arousal, you could start monitoring how – or whether – they change as the season progresses. Perhaps you prefer to be as relaxed as possible during the first few shows, in order to help your horses adjust and make them realise that 'going to a party' is nothing to get wound up about. As the weeks go by, and you and your horse get into the swing of things, you'll notice that now you actually need just that little bit more oomph to be at your best.

And what about any 'mitigating circumstances'? How does your life, your job, your family affect your ideal competitive arousal? Do you find that after a stressful week, you can only handle very little stress, yet when you're well rested, you're ready to take on the world? We'll discuss some of these elements in more detail when we talk about how to prepare for a competition in the third part of this book. Still, it's never too early to start thinking about it…

OPTIMISING YOURSELF

Right then. So once you've determined how much arousal you need, the next step is to get you there consistently. As you will undoubtedly have realised by now, getting yourself into the right frame of mind requires a combination of the right thoughts running through your head and physically feeling 'up for it'.

Let's have a look at how you might be able to manage the physical symptoms of your body. As the majority of problems are associated with trying to calm yourself, that's what we'll start with.

1. If all else fails, breathe!

Stress (whether physical or emotional) is often associated with what is commonly known as shallow or chest breathing. As you breathe in, your shoulders and collarbones rise up and your tummy muscles contract. As a result, the amount of air you inhale will be minimal, so you will have to breathe more quickly to supply your body with oxygen. The problem is, the faster you breathe, the more wound-up you'll feel.

103

Therefore, one of the most effective ways of dealing with an onslaught of the jitters is to slow and deepen your breathing (often referred to as 'deep' or 'abdominal' breathing). This will result in contractions of your diaphragm. (In fact, many people also refer to deep breathing as diaphragmatic breathing, but any yogi worth their rubber mat will tell you that there is a difference.) Instead of merely breathing into your chest, try to direct your breaths towards your abdomen. Your belly should expand as you breathe in. Hold your breath for a moment, then allow the air to be released. Your belly should contract as you do so. Preferably, exhalation should last about twice as long as inhalation, but you might need to practise for a bit before you are able to do this.

In essence, you are counteracting the body's automatic 'fight or flight' reaction, thus almost forcing your body to relax.

The neat thing? Deep, abdominal (or diaphragmatic) breathing can be done pretty much anywhere – even on top of your horse.

2. Find your centre

An exercise closely associated to deep breathing is 'centring' and will allow you to counteract both the physical tension associated with stress and any counterproductive thoughts running wild in your head. In any non-horsey sports setting, the initial steps would be to stand with your feet slightly apart and knees bent in order to prevent your knees locking and muscles becoming even stiffer. Obviously, if you're in the middle of a training session, or even a test, you might not want to get off. Luckily, the way we sit on our horses is a natural imitation of the 'centring stance', with our knees bent and shoulders, hips and heels aligned (ideally, anyway). So all you need to do now is to consciously relax your shoulders and neck. Open your mouth slightly (avoiding a tense jaw and grinding teeth!). Then, focus on breathing into your abdomen, allowing your tummy to expand as you do so. Hold your breath for a moment, then exhale, keeping as relaxed as possible through your upper body as you do so.

Doesn't sound too hard, does it?

And yet, as you 'centre' yourself, you'll be relaxing your body, while, at the same time, disrupting any negative, counterproductive stream of thought. In a way, you'll be able to 'reset' yourself, enabling you to start again. That's also why centring is effective in times when you've lost your focus, such as following a mistake.

3. Relax...progressively

Sometimes we're not even aware of how much tension we carry with us in our bodies. That's because, well, we just get used to it. Human beings are amazing at becoming accustomed to the most gruelling of circumstances, so a bit of physical tension has never done anybody any harm.

Err... Not quite. And especially not in horse sports.

Being able to ride effectively relies on what is called fine motor control. As you train your horse, you'll get him used to very subtle cues. Placing your leg one inch further back might mean sideways rather than forward. Opening your hand a fraction more might mean 'turn' rather than 'bend'. Unlike running, cycling, swimming or rowing, whereby larger muscle groups carry out most of the work, the kind of accuracy used in horse sports depends on the controlled co-ordination of small muscular movements. But the more tense you are, the more difficult it is to get this type of co-ordination right. The effect on the horse can be considerable. Think about it. A horse that is already highly strung and struggling to 'listen' to you, will only become more confused if the aids you are giving are not the same as the ones you give at home. Muscles that are rock solid from tension cannot give soft and subtle aids.

But – and this is the big but – in order to do something about it, you need to recognise it first. This is where progressive muscle relaxation comes in handy. Developed by the American physician Edmund Jacobson in the early 1920s, the technique helps to monitor and control tension in each specific muscle group.

Start out by lying flat on your back, arms and legs stretched out. Centre yourself by focusing on your breathing. Then, work through all your muscle groups one by one. Start with your feet. Tense them as much as you can and hold that tension up to a count of ten. Then release, and feel how your muscles relax. Enjoy the feeling of relaxation again up to a count of ten. Then shift your focus to your calf muscles. Repeat the exercise. First tense, then relax. Move your focus towards your thighs, then your buttocks, your back, your stomach, your upper arms, lower arms, hands, and finish up with your neck and facial muscles.

Once you're through, your body should feel entirely relaxed. What is more, you'll have taken the first steps towards recognising what it feels like to be very tense or very relaxed. As you practise, you'll quickly become an expert on recognising levels of tension in your muscles. Soon, you won't even need to tense your muscles anymore, but can progress to relaxing them immediately. At this point, you might even want to include a 'trigger' word, such as 'relax' or 'chill'. As we'll discuss later on, people are as good as horses in making connections. This is called classical conditioning (remember Pavlov and the dog and the bell?!). As long as you say the word slightly before you're about to relax, your body will soon learn, that that particular word does, indeed, mean relax!

Lastly, don't forget to start off with your breathing exercises. They'll set the scene and prepare you both physically and mentally.

After a while, you'll also be able to combine different muscle groups, so that in the end, running through a 'whole body check' should only take a few seconds.

PUTTING IT ALL TOGETHER

Imagine you're at a show. Perhaps you're in a situation similar to Roberta's. Perhaps normally you're the coolest competitor around, but this time, something's rattled you.

Whatever it is, you can feel your arousal level rise. What do you do? It's simple, really.

1. Listen to your body

What is it telling you? Is what you're feeling merely a sign that you're ready to compete? That body and mind have reached 'operating temperature'? Or are you feeling increasingly uncomfortable, and you're quickly approaching your danger zone?

2. Take a different perspective

This includes reminding yourself that you've got what it takes, that it's all about your own goals, and that there'll always be another show.

3. Centre yourself

Knees relaxed, shoulders relaxed. Then guide your focus towards your middle and…

4. Breathe

As you breathe into your abdomen, you'll be resetting body and mind. Any unwanted thoughts will be replaced with having to concentrate on the air flowing in and out of your lungs and belly.

5. Relax

Use your trigger word to let go of the superfluous tension in any or all of your muscles.

6. Use a pre-performance routine

A pre-performance routine constitutes a set order of behaviours, thoughts or actions that precede your actual performance. By sticking to exactly the same things you do at exactly the same time, you start to associate taking action with that particular sequence of events. What is more, you stop thinking and start doing (in essence, you are forming a 'habit' – check chapter 12 for more details). The more you use your pre-performance routine, the more your body will 'know' what's coming next and execute movements in the correct manner – which, obviously, is key to being able to perform consistently. What is more, because you know what's coming, it'll give you a definite sense of security. So how do you go about setting a routine? Thankfully, it's not actually all that complicated. All you need is a relevant trigger and several short behaviours executed in the same order that'll help you achieve the right frame of mind. It's important to remember that a simple routine can be as, or even more powerful, than a complex one. For example, as you're about to enter the ring, you could follow a simple relaxation routine involving:

1. your trigger, for example the word 'relax', followed by a series of behaviour, such as
2. taking a deep breath,
3. guide your attention to your tummy as you do (centring),
4. use a trigger word such as 'relax' or 'ready' (depending on what your optimal state of arousal is),
5. give the aid to trot or canter on.

You might also use a particular gesture or word to trigger your routine such as:

1. nod your head once to indicate (to yourself) that you're ready to commence. You'll continue with behaviours such as
2. breathe,
3. centre yourself,
4. use your trigger word,
5. give the aid to go.

Consider including a different trigger word to indicate what you should focus on or visualise yourself entering the arena or coming out of the starting box confidently. We'll discuss those techniques in the following chapters.

PSYCHING YOURSELF UP

Admittedly, it doesn't happen all that often, but there might be instances when you might need to psych yourself up, rather than calm yourself down. Perhaps you've had so much on your plate that you can't face another competition, but you've made yourself go anyway. But once there, you realise that you feel completely flat. So what do you do?

1. Listen to your favourite tune

That is, as long as your favourite tune is upbeat, positive and has a 'go get it' vibe to it. You'll know of course that music can and does have an influence on our emotions. So use it. Make yourself a play list with songs that cheer you up, give you energy and let you show your 'moves'.

2. Get physical...

... but only off the horse, please. Remember the bit about stress causing your body to respond with an increased heart and respiratory rate? Well, if you can't get yourself worked up (in a good way) about your show, then why not fake it? Run around the block (e.g. the lorry park) a few times. Do high jumps, punch the air, clap your hands, strut your stuff. It'll help you feel energised and, in turn, should raise that 'oomph' scale by a few points.

3. Talk yourself ready

The power of language is not to be underestimated. Think what happens at a big competition, when the entire audience stands up and cheers. Think what happens when your trainer is telling you to 'get a move on'. Exactly! The response is immediate. Lethargy disappears and you feel yourself becoming motivated once again. Stuck for things to say to yourself? What would you say if you wanted to get somebody going? Got it? Just do it!

4. Use a pre-performance routine

Pre-performance routines aren't merely useful to calm yourself down or to cope with anxiety. They can equally help gear you up. Obviously though, you'll need to change the tone and content of your routine ever so slightly. You might start off with an 'active' gesture and then amend your trigger word slightly (but I would suggest to stick with the breathing and centring, as that is as much about focus as it is about relaxation!). So you might:

1. do a thumbs up (you don't even have to let go of the contact for that – just raise your thumbs for a moment),
2. breathe,
3. centre yourself, and
4. use a trigger word to invoke a positive, confident mood, such as 'let's go!',
5. give the aid to 'let rip!'

Got it? Sure you do!

But if there's one key message to take away from this chapter, I guess it would be that pre-competitive anxiety is definitely not the evil it's often made out to be. In fact, if you learn to interpret those physical signs of arousal as your body's way of saying that you're ready, it'll become your very best friend.

In the words of Nick Burton:

'I would be more concerned about not feeling anxiety than feeling anxiety. So I expect it and I want it. So that I know that I am ready.'

TROUBLE SHOOTING

It is a truism in all sports that you'll compete how you train. And it holds true in horse sports too. You need to make sure that whatever you set out to do at a show you've practised at home. Remember, one of the things that causes anxiety is the idea that you might not be able to cope. Well, make sure you've covered your bases at home. If you know your horse spooks at flowerpots, get him used to flowerpots at home. If you know that your horse is alert to the point of being naughty outside, make sure you regularly train in an outside arena. Don't expect luck to be on your side when you're out competing, because chances are, it won't be.

Nick Burton agrees:

'Things going wrong is part of a competition. I should expect it rather than be surprised by it. So that's how I deal with it –

I expect it at some point to go wrong and that then I am equipped to deal with it rather than going "aw why did that happen; why did that go wrong?"

So really, it's all about expecting that things change or go wrong or fall down or whatever, rather than saying "oh why has this gone wrong, I am not prepared to cope with that".'

The answer?

Be as prepared as humanly possible.

But sometimes, all the preparation in the world isn't going to help you when you get an attack of the nerves... Suddenly, the proverbial monster is lurking behind every single proverbial bush. The brave lion you set out to be turns into a frightened rabbit.

When anxious, we're inclined to lose all perspective. All of a sudden, we're worth nothing. We can't do anything. And we certainly don't belong here. As tempting as it is then to give in, throw in the towel and go home, my advice would be... just don't!

Take a step back. Figuratively and literally. First of all, try to look at the situation from an outside perspective. How would someone else judge your situation? Would they agree that you're in over your head? If it's easier, imagine you're your own best friend. What would she or he say? Talk yourself through all the things you've done in training to get you this far. Are you still convinced you're not able to cope?

Use your favourite technique to calm yourself. Managed to get your anxiety down a notch or two? Got closer to your optimal level? Great! Give yourself a pat on the back for that. Now all you need to remind yourself is that this is just another signal for you to go and compete. Quite clearly, your body is over-eager today.

So just go and do your thing!

CHAPTER 9

FOCUS: RIDING IN FLOW

As far as show jumping competitions go, the Longines Global Champions Tour, or LGCT as the series is also affectionately known, is quite something to behold. In 2006, Jan Tops, former show jumper, winner of countless championship titles, including Team Gold at the 1992 Barcelona Olympics, decided to 'up the ante' in international show jumping by founding the Global Champions Tour series. Today, the starter list at every show reads like the 'who's who' of equestrian nobility, with Olympic, World and European champions battling it out for the top prize. Locations such as Chantilly, Monaco and Shanghai range from exclusive to luxurious. VIP guests regularly include the rich and famous such as H.S.H. Prince Albert II of Monaco, Princess Caroline of Hanover, Sir Roger Moore, and Bruce Springsteen. And to top it all off the season prize money total lies at around €9 million.

Enough glitz, glamour and high society to distract even the most seasoned of campaigners! But not Gregory Wathelet.

On Friday, 4th July 2014, the Belgian Olympian entered the 1.50 m Gucci-sponsored Prix du Qatar on his nine-year old bay stallion Conrad de Hus. The class was a qualifying round for the LGCT Grand Prix the following day. It would be somewhat of an understatement to say there was something at stake.

But horse and rider looked the picture of harmony and control, with Conrad de Hus cantering in a lovely rhythm and outline, clearing jump after jump with ease.

Until fence number 9.

Suddenly, in mid-air, the entire bridle started slipping over the stallion's ears. A couple of strides later, and it dangled off his nose, with only the bit still left in his mouth.

What did Gregory Wathelet do?

He carried on as if nothing had happened. He kept a hold on

the contact, barely wavered in his rhythm and guided his horse over the remaining three fences, dropping not a single pole.

Having crossed the finishing line, he asked his horse to walk (a straight transition from canter no less), and jumped out of the saddle. The most astonishing thing? His features maintained the same expression throughout. Not a flicker of annoyance at his mishap or relief at this equestrian masterpiece. Nothing but focus.

Focus on what matters.

Focus on the job at hand.

Focus on the moment.

RIDING IN FLOW

It's what riders dream off. That one round, one test, where concentration is so complete that everything else fades in the background (even a lost bridle!). Only one thought, one feeling dominates. If only that one moment would last for all eternity.

I bet you know precisely what I'm talking about. It might have happened in training or in competition, while out hacking, or galloping across the beach. Whatever the occasion, the feelings would have been the same. Immersed in the here and now, you would have felt absolutely in control. You would have felt that anything and everything was possible.

Most importantly, the feeling of satisfaction, of elation, of utter bliss afterwards, makes it one of the most addictive experiences in sport (and life).

This amazing and widely coveted mental state has been called all sorts of things. Focus. Optimal concentration. Being in the zone (which also partly related to physical arousal, which just goes to show how closely the two concepts are related). By the way, depending on who talks about it, details might differ marginally, but essentially it all boils down to the same principles.

The famed psychology professor with the unpronounceable name, Mihály Csíkszentmihályi calls it 'flow'. When interviewing research subjects about their experiences with absolute focus they kept describing the experience as being carried along by water. Thus the term 'flow' was born.

113

Anyway, as a Hungarian scientist who emigrated to the US at the tender age of 22, Csíkszentmihályi spent most of his career researching the concepts of happiness, motivation and concentration. Intrigued by artists so engrossed in their work that they would forego even the most basic needs such as food, water and sleep, Csíkszentmihályi developed his key theories on flow in the 1980s and 1990s, and he and fellow researchers have expanded on them since. As a result, we now know that 'flow' in all its effortless glory encompasses several important features.[64]

1. Challenge yourself

First of all, you need to feel like you're being challenged. At the same time, you need to believe you've got what it takes to succeed. Note the word 'believe' – in sport psychology circles, this is called 'perceived skill level'. Actually having the necessary skills is, of course, a bonus, but believing you do is even more important. That is how people rise above themselves. By believing they can. You've probably spotted it already, but this idea that you need to challenge yourself is in line with goal-setting principles: more challenging goals lead to improved performance. You're only going to make a real effort if you feel like you're being stretched.

2. The here and now

Your entire being needs to be focused on the here and now. No thinking of what happened yesterday (or even five minutes ago) or what might happen tomorrow (or in ten seconds' time). This is what Gregory Wathelet must have felt. Even though he noticed the bridle coming off, instead of being paralysed by a thought such as 'oh no, what now?', he simply kept going, doing what he was doing. No analysis of how it might have happened, how it made him look as a rider (amazing, actually) or what to do in future.

---

64   Nakamura, J., and Csíkszentmihályi, M. (20th December 2001), 'Flow Theory and Research', in C.R. Snyder Erik Wright, and Lopez, S.J., *Handbook of Positive Psychology*, Oxford University Press, pp. 195–206, ISBN 978-0-19-803094-2. Retrieved 20th November 2013

3. Action = awareness

Then, action and awareness must merge. Behaviour must become thought, and thought must become behaviour. Simply put, whatever you think, you do; whatever you do, you think. Quite often, this state of affairs has been referred to as the horse being able to read your mind. Rather than any supernatural cognitive abilities on the part of your four-legged friend, this is simply you being so tuned into your riding, that as you're thinking of, say, an aid to canter, your body's already doing it. And the horse responds.

4. Shut up!

Or, more politely put, reflective self-consciousness recedes into the background. Instead of being continuously, and often uncomfortably, preoccupied with yourself, your actions, and what you or others might think of them, you simple are. No preconceptions, no judgement. Ever been so focused on your horse, that you didn't notice a friend, trainer, spouse trying to get your attention even though you're usually the first to realise if someone's watching you? Ever experienced something like that? That's what it's like to switch off that inner critique.

5. Control

What's more, you feel in control. You become the sole driving force behind all of your actions at that particular moment in time. (Remember the bit about autonomy being an intrinsic need? Here it is again.) Again, that feeling of literally being one with your horse, of your horse reacting instantaneously to your every command, is a pretty good description of what absolute control feels like. There's no fear, no doubt. There's just riding.

6. Want it!

Not surprisingly perhaps, in order to experience true flow, whatever it is you're doing must feel intrinsically rewarding. Now we're (almost) back to where we started. Whatever you're doing, you must really want to do it. It must be part of who you are, and what you want from life.

7.   There's no such thing as time

Time stands still. Or speeds up. Or seems to be doing both. One thing that is certain is that the subjective experience of time alters considerably. That one's easy. You've planned to ride for 40 minutes, and by the time you stop it's over an hour gone… Well, they don't say 'time flies if you're having fun' for nothing…

Sounds great, doesn't it? But all you'll want to know is how to do it yourself. Right now!

First of all, the common reprimand, so loved by teachers, instructors and coaches all across the world, 'You're not concentrating,' doesn't exist. We're always concentrating. Just not always on the right thing.

Irritating? Absolutely! But there's a reason for it.

KNOW YOUR FOCUS

At any given moment, no matter where you are or what you are doing, countless bits of information clamour for your attention, demanding to be addressed. From an evolutionary perspective, learning which ones to address and which ones to ignore could have made the difference between survival and certain death (imagine the consequences of ignoring a mountain lion waiting to pounce…). In today's westernised world, where being attacked by wild animals only forms the most marginal of threats, there's still plenty to catch our eye (both figuratively and literally), including overcrowded motorways with dare-devil drivers and endless demands from Twitter, Facebook and co.

Even in the relatively contained environment of a training session with your horse, there'll be a myriad of sensations flooding your visual cortex and demanding your attention.

Imagine you're warming up your horse in the outdoor arena. First off, there's the weather. Is it hot, is it cool, does it rain, is it cloudy or windy?

Might your horse react differently? If so, how are you going to react? Then there's your immediate surroundings, such as trees, bushes, perhaps a stream. Any wildlife contained in it? Any birds ready to be startled, ducks to take their daily bath, bunnies to pretend they're horse-eating monsters. And what about insects, flies, gnats, horse-flies? What about the surface. If the sun's been beating down for days, it might be very dusty. Working your horse long and low might cause him to cough and sneeze. It might be bone dry and hard, causing jarring in his legs. If it's been raining instead of sunny, puddles of water might have turned the arena into an obstacle course. If you're about to have a lesson, you're trainer might already be standing in the middle, giving initial instructions. Sit up, look up, walk forward, slow down. Perhaps your best friend is leaning against the fence, watching you. She's recently lost her horse so you feel really sorry for her. What might she be thinking now? Or, instead of your friend, it might be your arch-enemy. She owns the most expensive horse at the yard and pretends she knows everything there is to know about horse riding. Her arms are crossed, her body rigid. She's probably hoping you'll do a really bad job. Or so you think.

And this is only in training. Imagine what happens in competition. There'll be flags, flowers, tents, spectators, judges, other competitors, people you might wish to impress such as sponsors or owners – all vying for your attention.

A seemingly endless list and we haven't even so much as mentioned those elements instrumental to how you'll perform in the saddle – namely you and your horse.

No wonder it can be so difficult to achieve a state of perfect focus. There's simply too much information!

What's worse, in times of stress or anxiety, especially when you're lacking in confidence or when you are more concerned with the outcome of a competition (e.g. ego-orientation), your focus will be irrevocably drawn to exactly those elements that secretly – or not so secretly – worry you. That judge, for example. He might give you a lower score than you think you deserve. Or that other competitor. Her horse is much better than yours, isn't it? In fact, quite often, the more anxious you get, the more your focus will start shifting from one worrying distraction to another. Once again, from an evolutionary perspective this might once have been a useful trait. If you're worried about being eaten by a mountain lion, it's a good idea to keep checking that those rustling leaves over there aren't actually camouflaging a mountain lion… Nevertheless, you'll probably agree that at a modern day horse show focusing on everything but your horse isn't conducive to optimal performance.

And yet, during those precious moments when you actually manage to enter 'the zone' or 'flow', your focus will narrow to the point of blocking out all unwanted, unnecessary stimuli. You are able to pay what is called selective attention to aspects of your performance that will help you succeed.

It's precisely what Pippa Funnell managed to pull off at the 1999 European Championships in Luhmühlen. Against all odds, too. In fact, in her autobiography, she confessed to the following:

'I have never felt pressure and nervousness like I felt in Luhmühlen.' [65]

The reason? When Pippa was picked for the team with her bay gelding Supreme Rock, not everyone in the sport applauded the decision of the Chairman of the Selection Committee. Pippa was untested at international senior level and Luhmühlen was the final opportunity for the British to qualify for the Sydney Olympics the following year. Imagine an Olympic Games without a British eventing team. It would have been unheard of…

Yet after a superb dressage and clear cross-country, Pippa found herself the overnight leader with only the show jumping to go.

'(…) I only had two fences in hand to win the individual gold over the Swedish rider, Linda Algotsson, who is very good at show jumping. William (Funnell, Pippa's husband) helped me warm up and I tried to keep my head and stay focused. I had to remember I was there to do a job and ride Rocky in the way William and I had worked on. … with Rocky, the rhythm has

---

65   Funnell, P. (2005), *The Autobiography*, London, Orion Books

to be slower than for most horses; you have to keep him soft, ride with little leg, keep him as relaxed as possible and not thrust him deep to fences.' [66]

She ended up winning the gold medal. She did this by narrowing her focus to the one thing that mattered. How to ride Rocky.

Pippa Funnell and Gregory Wathelet demonstrate very aptly what happens when you're able to focus on just the things that matter. What is more, they also demonstrate that a) You can choose to focus, and b) You can shift your focus.

In many ways focusing is like using the beam of a torch to light up whatever it is you wish to see. If you need more information, for example about the environment you are going to be riding in, you simply broaden your beam. That way, you can take in as much as you need and plan accordingly. If, however, you have your plan in place, and now want to shut out irrelevant details or distractions, you simply narrow your beam, focusing it onto just those elements you need.

Professor Dr Robert Nideffer, Department Head at the School of Humanities, Arts, and Social Sciences at the Rensselaer Polytechnic Institute, developed an entire theory around attentional styles that explains this concept of widening and narrowing your focus in much more detail. In fact, Nideffer argues that attention (focus) travels on two independent dimensions. One is width, the other direction.

Specifically, attentional width involves individuals being able to shift their focus from very broad, taking in lots of their environment, but losing out on specific detail, to very narrow, whereby they hone in on just one element, but take in all of its specifics.

Attentional direction on the other hand is all about whether athletes focus externally, on their environment, or internally, on their own thoughts or feelings. A diagram including all four attentional styles would look like this:

66   Funnell, P. (2005), *The Autobiography*, London, Orion Books

	EXTERNAL	INTERNAL
BROAD	An external-broad attentional style means taking in most or all of your surroundings. You won't be able to take in much detail, but you'll miss very little of what's going on.	An internal-broad attention style involves lots of thinking, making plans, critically analysing a situation. It's all about your thoughts.
NARROW	An external-narrow attentional style means focusing on one object in your surroundings (including your horse) and ignoring everything else. Narrowing your focus also means being able to take in much more detail.	An internal-narrow attentional style means paying attention to only one or two thoughts or feelings at any one time. Everything else becomes unimportant.

So here's the good news: People can take the conscious decision to shift their focus. They can predetermine which bits of information are worthy of their attention and which ones they should ignore. They can choose their relevant attentional style depending on the demands of the situation. If you are a show jumper, an eventer, an individual vaulter, a dressage or Western rider, your focus needs to be narrow most of the time, focusing on just those elements that are instrumental to your and your horse's performance. It's what Pippa did in that fateful show jumping round that secured her the European gold medal:

> '...with Rocky, the rhythm has to be slower than for most horses; you have to keep him soft, ride with little leg, keep him as relaxed as possible and not thrust him deep to fences.'[67]

---

67   Funnell, P. (2005), *The Autobiography*, London, Orion Books

If you are a polo or horse ball player, a team vaulter, a jockey or endurance rider, your focus would generally have to be broader. While there might be times when you need to 'hone' back in on yourself, the horse, or other, single elements such as the ball, your primary modus of attention should be broad, taking in the positions of other players, team mates or competitors.

The direction your focus will take also depends on what you've identified as vital elements to achieve peak performance. If you know that your horse responds best when you remain as relaxed as possible, your focus is likely to be internal. If keeping a good rhythm is the key to success, you might need to focus externally on your horse. It goes without saying that seeing a stride or aiming for the middle of a fence are also external points of focus.

Perhaps you've realised it already, but I'll say it anyway: sometimes we get caught in an attentional style that is not conducive to performance. For example, if you're in the middle of a dressage test, and suddenly you start over-analysing your performance, or what the judge might think, or what you're planning to have for tea that night, you'll be unlikely to perform very well. All the more important to narrow your focus back down to what matters most. Or you might be in the correct attentional style but focusing on the wrong thing. If you are in the middle of a polo match, and should really be keeping an eye on the opposing team, but are side-tracked by the pretty ladies milling about at the edge of the field, you're also not likely to do very well – even though you were already engaged in the – correct – externally broad focus. Time to shift your focus to what matters most!

In essence though, identifying which elements are important shouldn't be all that difficult. Not after you've spent time profiling your performance (see chapter 7) and mapping out which elements are most important.

So once you know what your main focus is going to be (broad or narrow, external or internal), you then need to allow your body to do its thing. Because once you've mastered a skill, e.g. your riding, and you're in flow, you shouldn't really have to think too much. Your body knows. You've practised for so long, your skills have become automated. Think of how you ask your horse to canter. Usually you'd make sure that your horse is engaged and listening to your aids, and then… you just, well, canter… No need to think of the specifics. Your body acts automatically. And so it should. Believe in that.

Obviously, this is different when you've only just started riding. At that point, you rely on what is called controlled processing of information. You need to attend to all the different aids. Your out-side leg, your inside leg. The slight shift of your weight. Asking your horse to bend ever so slightly to the inside. It all takes longer, is less smooth and might mean your horse might first trot faster or throw its head up simply because your aids aren't as well timed. But that's perfectly okay. It's just a question of keeping up your practice, and your skills become automated all by themselves.

Assuming, though, that you're at the automatic stage, all you should want to do is identify what you want to do – and then allow your body to take over. It's a vital component of being able to get 'in the zone' or 'in flow'.

ACHIEVING FLOW

Right then, we've pretty much come full circle. Let's put all the ingredients together to achieve perfect focus. Flow. The zone.

1. Know what to do

Everything keeps coming back to this one vital first step. Know what you want to do. Set the right kind of goals. When we're talking concentration though, it's not so much about your long-term goals (even though they should be at the back of your mind), but more your short-term, process-orientated goals. What do you need to do to ensure that you and your horse perform?

2. Make it challenging

Stretch yourself a little. Go the extra mile. It doesn't matter how you put it, you need to feel that whatever you do is just outside your comfort zone. Note the word just. It moves us onto the next point…

3. Believe that you can do it

It's all about the perception of your own ability. If you've done your homework and you've mapped out your path, in a realistic, SMART, manner, you can feel confident that it's all good. If you still doubt yourself though, check how far you've come already and remind yourself of all the other challenges you've met in the past.

4. Optimal arousal

Make sure you're in your optimal zone of 'oomph', e.g. not too tense, not too relaxed (see the previous chapter). Being physically ready and able to keep pre-competitive nerves in perspective is another important pre-condition for developing the right focus.

5. No distractions

Being in flow means focusing on just what matters, nothing else. Sometimes, that can be easier said than done. Remember though that ego-involvement (e.g. focusing on winning or comparing yourself with others) will encourage you to focus on those around you rather than yourself. Therefore, try and be task-involved. As selfish as it may sound, make it all about you and your horse. Focus on actions, not results!

6. Decide to concentrate

Make it a conscious decision. It works like a reminder to yourself to get yourself in the correct frame of mind. Remember that focusing on the right thing doesn't just happen by accident (at least not most of the time).

7. Centre yourself

If you've read the previous chapter, you'll know about this already. The simple act of focusing on relaxing your body and breathing into your abdomen will stop any disruptive thoughts, effectively emptying your mind. It allows you to start with a 'clean slate' as you focus on what matters most.

8. Use a trigger word

Again, this'll sound familiar. Human beings learn by association. Do two things together often enough and, after a while, your body will remember. As you can use a trigger to stimulate relaxation, you can also choose a trigger word to initiate the right kind of focus which can really help you in the long run. Your trigger word could either be generic, something like 'focus', or more specific, for example a description on what you've set yourself to do, e.g. 'rhythm'. Better still, if your trigger word reflects the type of attentional style you're after. You might choose to tell yourself 'wide' or 'opponent', if you're in the middle of a polo match and you should really be focusing externally and broad. Or you're approaching a fence and need an externally-narrow type of focus. Think 'ahead' or 'tunnel vision'. If you've sat down to map out your competition strategy for the coming month, but you find yourself staring at the TV instead, you might tell yourself to 'plan' or 'reflect' (and turn off the TV!). Lastly, if the attentional focus you're after is internal narrow, use relevant words to hone in on what you should be focusing on, e.g. 'feel' or 'soft'.

9. Use a routine

As much as you can teach your body to adopt optimal levels of arousal by using a routine (see the previous chapter), you can also teach your body to focus. In fact, the two concepts are very closely related, so you might as well make use of the same principle, or better still, combine your two routines to get yourself in the right state of arousal and focus (seeing that they are so closely related). Remember, a routine is all about security and not having to worry what to do next.

10. Trust your body

You know how to ride. You know what you've set yourself to do. You've developed triggers to initiate the right kind of focus. Now allow your body to do its thing.

TROUBLE SHOOTING

All right. Now you know how to achieve your optimal concentration. You'll know how to get into your 'zone', your 'flow'. You've got your plan. You've set your goals. You know what you need to do, and believe that, in fact, you *can* do it. You've used your trigger word and your routine.

But the people around you simply don't get it. They expect you still to be able to answer your phone or send a quick text while trying to train. Or they really want you to stop and chat while on the way to the warm-up at a show. You try to explain, but all you get are blank looks. Surely you should be able to do it all at once...

One of the most common misconceptions of the 21st century is that doing several things at once is a sign of great productivity. To get to the top, or so people think, you need to be able to multitask. Well, they're wrong.

Multitasking doesn't work. We just think it does, because we merely think we're being productive, while in fact, we're not actually doing anything properly.

Here's why. Early research by Csíkszentmihályi[68] has shown that the amount of information we can focus on effectively at one particular moment in time is, in fact, really rather limited. More specifically, 126 bits of information per second. Even though at first glance this might sound like quite a lot, engaging in a simple conversation already takes up 40 bits – one-third of total capacity, of available brain space – leaving considerably fewer resources to focus on other tasks. In fact, recent research, by Dr Clifford Nass, Professor of Communication at the University of Stanford[69] , showed that contrary to popular belief, 'multi-tasking' doesn't lead to greater productivity or performance. People are, in fact, unable to

---

68 Csíkszentmihályi, M. (1988), 'The flow experience and its significance for human psychology', in Csíkszentmihályi, M., *Optimal experience: psychological studies of flow in consciousness*, Cambridge, Cambridge University Press, pp. 15–35, ISBN 978-0-521-43809-4

69 http://news.stanford.edu/news/2009/august24/multitask-research-study-082409.html

perform several activities at the same time. Those who try, end up much worse and will, without fail, be outperformed by individuals who are able to focus on only one thing at a time.

So next time someone tries to get you to do something else when you're just about to focus, just tell them that bit of interesting trivia. And in case they're not impressed, or just don't believe you, tell them you're taking your cue from show jumping Olympian Janne-Friederike Meyer. She is known for never talking on the phone while riding.

> 'Quite a few people don't like that about me because I am very difficult to reach, but I like doing one thing at a time if it is important.' [70]

But what if you lose it? What if you were all focused and things were going incredibly well, and then, suddenly, something happens? Your telephone rings, someone insists on talking to you, a loose horse canters by or a dog runs across the track. You might get a serious attack of the jitters. Or things are going so well that you're overcome by feelings of happiness. And yes, just before you ask – positive emotions are actually as much of a distraction as negative ones.

As a result, you make a mistake. Because you've made that one mistake, suddenly you're floundering. So you'll make another. And another.

The reason? You guessed it! You've lost your focus. Here's the thing. It's perfectly normal and will have happened to just about everyone. The key is to not panic, but to keep doing precisely what you've done before. Remind yourself of your goal. Consciously set your mind to focusing again. Centre your body. Use your trigger. Use your routine. And believe.

In the words of Mary King:

> 'You have to try and not dwell on it, try and keep concentrating on what's ahead and not be thinking about a mistake you've just made.'

---

70   Kreling, K. (2012), 'Germany's Got Talent', *Horse Sport International*, Issue 3

CHAPTER 10

SELF-TALK: REANALYSE, REFRAME, RETHINK

I t's the first time you're about to compete at the European Championships. In fact, it's the first time you're officially representing your country at a major championship. It still feels somewhat unreal, driving in the team bus, surrounded by all the other team members. The national trainer is being really nice to you and the reigning world champion, someone you've looked up to for as long as you can remember, has been assigned to be at your side throughout the competition.

You arrive at the competition and settle in as best as you can.

The day of the first test arrives. You get yourself and your horse ready and do your warm-up. So far, so good.

You've got two minutes to go. You think you're ready. As ready as you'll ever be, anyway.

And suddenly, out of the blue, your trousers split. Right down the middle. There's no way you can compete like that.

Or is there?

A nightmare scenario for any competitor, to be sure. But it's unlikely to happen, right?

Wrong!

This is exactly what happened to German vaulter Viktor Brüsewitz at the Junior European Championships in Brno, Czech Republic, in 2008.

As he was about to enter the arena to perform his compulsory exercises, his unitard ripped right down the middle. With only seconds to spare he threw on the unitard he'd borrowed from a fellow competitor, then raced towards the arena.

What happened next?

Did he lose his focus? Was he so rattled that he was unable to show what he was capable of? Did thoughts like 'How could this have happened?'

or 'This isn't fair?' or, worse, 'What an idiot I am to let this happen.'

Nope. None of the above. Instead, Viktor thought,

'Now we'll show them how it's done.'

And he did, going into the lead with 0.2 point. He kept it too, right up until the last day, where a minor mistake cost him the gold medal by 0.0005 point.

Even though Viktor went home with 'only' a silver medal, he proved, at the tender age of 18, what it means to keep your cool under pressure and your thoughts under control.

Self-talk. The voice inside your head. Your constant companion. Virtually impossible to shut up, difficult to control, but oh so important to achieving your optimal frame of mind. Think about it.

As you ride (or, in fact, whenever you do pretty much anything) you are continuously giving yourself instructions, praising or criticising, commenting on or evaluating what is going on. Any of these thoughts are likely to have an impact on how you feel. If you are positive, you are likely to feel okay, too. Equally, if you're criticising yourself harshly, your mood is likely to plummet. In turn, you might then do something that causes your horse to be tense or jump about. Chances are you'll have realised that your own actions caused your horse to misbehave, and you'll feel even worse, criticising yourself even more harshly. A vicious circle, that can be tricky to break. At the same time, it also works the other way round. Positive comments often result in a better mood resulting in more constructive behaviour. Or a better mood results in more positive comments. Or effective behaviour results in positive commentary and then in a positive mood.

This interconnectedness of thoughts, feelings and emotions is often referred to as the cognitive triangle, and explains why it is so important to spend a little more time exploring what you think and say to yourself while you ride.

By the way, you're not the only one who this happens to nor is talking to yourself the first sign of madness!

THE WHERE, WHEN, WHAT AND WHY OF SELF-TALK

In fact, sport psychology researchers have known for some time that athletes tend to talk to themselves while engaged in their sport. As the effect on performance can be considerable, they have gone out of their way to explore it in more detail.

Together with several colleagues, one of the most prominent researchers in the field, Dr James Hardy, from the School of Sport, Health and Exercise Sciences at the University of Bangor, has defined self-talk as an overt (e.g. out loud) or covert (in your head) means to interpret sports-related ideas, feelings, perceptions or convictions.[71]

The '4 Ws' of self-talk discuss the where, when, what and why athletes might talk to themselves.

The Where

We now know that this more or less relentless stream of commentary in your head occurs both in training and in competition. In fact, it's there most of the time, but to classify as 'proper' self-talk, e.g. as something that helps your performance, it really needs to occur whenever you are performing or preparing to perform. Leading neatly onto…

The When

Whenever you are involved with your sport, two weeks in advance of a competition, as you're about to get onto your horse, or as you are actively engaged – or even once you're done and getting yourself ready for the next time.

The What

Depending on how things are going, what kind of mood you are in, your

71   Hardy, J., Gammage, K., and Hall, C. (2001), 'A descriptive study of athlete self-talk', *The Sport Psychologist*, pp. 15, 306-318

usual thought patterns, and what has gone on before, the things you say to yourself will either be positive or negative. In sport psychology terms,

1. Positive self-talk will be classified as statements that are encouraging, affirmative and/or instructive.
2. Negative self-talk is offensive, demeaning and/or critical without being constructive.

But – and this obviously won't come as a surprise – in order to enhance your performance, what you say to yourself must be positive. It should make you feel better or help you rather than make you feel bad or undermine your performance. Still, there are different options to what you might decide to say to yourself.

1. Give yourself specific instructions

If you've spent time setting your goals, you'll probably know by now what your process goals should be. As a reminder, process goals are what you need to do in order to achieve your desired performance. They need to be as specific as you can make them. They also shouldn't revolve around more than one or two elements, otherwise it'll be far too much to remember in any specific situation. So then, if you've got your process goals, why not incorporate them into your self-talk? That way, you'll continuously remind yourself what you should be focusing on. And it really is as simple as 'leg on' or 'soft hand' or 'sit tall' – if, of course, that is what you need to do to get your horse going.

Incidentally, it is vitally important that you phrase all instructions in a positive way. And no, I don't mean that kind of positive. I'm talking *language* here.

For example, what happens if I ask you to not think of a pink elephant?

Exactly! You'll think of nothing *but* a pink elephant!

So, in self-talk terms this means avoiding words such as 'not' and 'no'. Because by telling yourself that you shouldn't do this and that, you're essentially still encouraging your brain to register the actual activity – more importantly, as you're not providing your head and body with a valid alternative to what you should be doing, you're likely to end up doing exactly what you were trying to avoid.

2. Motivate yourself

Sometimes life as a rider is tough. Things go wrong, you're exhausted, your horse isn't doing what you want him to, in fact, the entire world seems to be conspiring against you.

But you know that you need to keep going. Of course you do. But it's so hard… That's where motivational self-talk comes in. These are words that are meant to encourage you, both in the long term or right there, in the ring. Words such as 'Come on!', 'You can do it', or, for Barack Obama fans 'Yes, we can!'.

3. Get in the mood

We'll talk more about establishing your most effective mood profile a little later on. Still, you'll know by now that getting yourself in the right kind of physical state is important to your performance. You also know that a trigger word can help you do that (see chapter 8 and 9). A trigger word such as 'Relax,' or 'Chill', or, when you need a little more 'oomph', 'Get ready!'.

The Why

And even though it's more important that self-talk does work, it's always fun, or at least interesting, to know how it works. It might just give that extra bit of motivation to go and try it…

1. Self-talk reduces interfering thoughts

The human brain can only process so much information at any given time. And don't forget, even though, ideally, much of your physical performance should be automated, your brain still needs processing space. Imagine your head is cluttered up with unnecessary streams of thoughts. The result?

You are unlikely to perform well, because all these thoughts are essentially distracting your brain from the job at hand (e.g. performing). Having just one key message to focus on will reduce the chatter, and free up brain space for the actual task.

2. It helps to initiate flow

Not only can self-talk help to keep any verbal distractions in your head to a minimum, thus freeing up space to concentrate on the important things, it can even help to initiate that coveted mental state. Flow. Remember? In order to get into that right state of mind, you need to know what to do. That's your (slightly challenging) process goal. Then you consciously decide to concentrate. Then you centre yourself. And then… you only allow that single thought to enter your consciousness. So then, self-talk can effectively act as your trigger for flow (as well as be a useful tool to remind you of what to do, to motivate yourself, and to put yourself in the right mood of course).

3. It activates your oomph score

By now you should know, or at least have a general idea, of your personal zone of optimal functioning. Remember? Your own 'oomph' score. Feeling 'just right' physically means having the confidence to tackle whatever challenge lies ahead. Self-talk can help you get there – as long as you know of course whether you need to calm yourself or gear yourself up. Over to you!

4. It increases confidence

Confidence is all about thinking that you've got the necessary skills you need to cope with a situation. But sometimes we tend to 'forget' all the things we can do. In all the excitement you suddenly can't remember that, really, you've jumped that kind of fence about a hundred times in practice or that you've practised that test (or relevant parts of it) until blue in the face. This is where self-talk can really make a difference. Talk yourself through that last successful round. Remind yourself of how you managed to tackle those flying changes, that half-pass or shoulder-in. Suddenly, your actual level of skill will keep coming back to you, and the challenge ahead won't seem quite so scary.

So then, teaching yourself to use the right words at the right time can make a big difference. Here's what top class eventer, Pippa Funnell, had to say about learning how phrasing those words in her head in a positive manner made a big difference:

> *'The word "not" is bad for my mental state and was banned by Nicky Heath (Pippa's sport psychologist), whose insistence that all instructions must be positive was one of the big lessons that turned my career around.'* [72]

And yet, so many riders still struggle with keeping their thoughts in line and positive. Why is that? In simple terms, because whenever we're worried, unsure, under pressure, not in flow or not feeling well, our attention is drawn towards whatever we perceive as a potential threat to our health or ego (and, yes, we've discussed this before). Your immediate response is to comment on it, and even though it is definitely more helpful or constructive to be positive, negative commentary might often serve as affirmation of what you were already thinking of yourself.

Sound crazy? Perhaps. But it really isn't.

RETHINK YOUR THOUGHTS

We live in a society that likes to think in absolutes. We like to categorise and stereotype. Good is good and bad is bad. Black is black and white is white. There's no in between, there're no shades of grey. We do this because it's easier and faster. Life is already complex enough as it is. So much information to take in, make decisions about, assess and react upon. If it's possible to categorise in order to make decision-making processes slightly

---

72   Funnell, P. (2005), *The Autobiography,* London, Orion Books

easier, then, generally, we jump at the chance. This kind of categorical thinking has helped mankind to survive, by reacting quickly and decisively, so it's not all bad.

But sometimes, thought patterns that categorise, label, and only ever tend to go in one direction, can wreak havoc with your emotional state of mind (and subsequent behaviour). In simple terms, they can really sabotage your attempts to reach a long-term goal because you'll end up struggling to consistently rephrase your self-talk in a positive manner – which, in turn, will impact negatively on your performance.

In fact, there are a number of thought patterns that might trap us in such a way. See whether you recognise yourself in one or several of them.

1. Perfectionist or all-or-nothing thinking

Favourite saying: 'I must be perfect, nothing else is good enough,' or 'If I'm not going to be the best, I won't bother.'

Perfectionist thinkers do not allow compromises, especially not when it's about their own level of performance. The problem, of course, is that we're all human, and being perfect all of the time is pretty much impossible to achieve. And come to think of it, whose definition of perfect are we talking, anyway…

What's more, even if you are very, very good, at some point there is going to be someone else who's going to be better than you. If you need an example, think of Isabell Werth, Anky van Grunsven, Edward Gal, Adelinde Cornelissen or Charlotte Dujardin. At some point, they were all winning one competition after the other. They seemed unbeatable. Until they *were* beaten. The notion of ultimate success is even more fleeting in most of the other disciplines. Expecting yourself to be perfect or the best all of the time, means you'll lose out on a lot of the enjoyment that goes into simply doing it for the fun of it.

2. Should statements

Favourite saying: 'I should have been able to ride that horse,' or 'My trainer should be helping me more.'

Using should statements essentially implies criticism, and unnecessary or unfair criticism at that. First of all, ask yourself by whose standards should you do anything? By your own, or someone else's? If you are trying to live up to other people's expectations, you need to ask yourself whether they conform to your own. If they do, and you agree that you need to handle a situation differently, develop relevant coping strategies. Take action. Set goals. Discuss with others. If, however, you realise that your (or other people's) expectations are, in fact, unreasonable… well, stop beating yourself up about it.

3. Over-personalisation

Favourite saying: 'It's my fault my student didn't ride well today. I should have taught him/her better,' or 'That guy's comment about bad riders – that was about me.'

Over-personalising means that you feel responsible for everyone else's problems – and are convinced that everyone has nothing better to do than talk, or rather criticise, you. Essentially you believe the world revolves around you, but not in a good way. Quite to the contrary, you think you should have all the answers and solutions. But by adopting the role of Superman, you deny that others are responsible for their own actions – and that the environment has got a lot to do with how things play out.

4. Selective attention or filtering

Favourite saying: 'Because of that one (tiny) mistake, the test was awful.' 'The fact that I jumped clear was pure luck.'

Do you tend to focus only on the negatives and diminish or even negate the positives in your riding (or your life)? Then you're likely a 'filterer', meaning that you go out of your way to search for things that go wrong. It's almost as if you're trying to say, 'look, my life (horse; riding skills, etc.) is rubbish, and here's proof'. In many ways, you might even feel satisfied, because at least you've managed to prove yourself right. But – continuously focusing on the negatives is incredibly draining and you are likely to end up in a downright spiral, where you don't believe in anything positive that might happen to you. How about turning it around, and looking for positives instead? Make it a habit to write down one thing that went well during the course of your day, and you'll soon notice a shift in perception.

5. Denial or blaming

Favourite saying: 'It wasn't my fault. My horse is just so naughty.'

Unfortunately, there are still quite a few riders out there who tend to blame their horse rather than take responsibility for their own actions. But failing to take responsibility or assigning blame to external sources will only result in you not taking the necessary steps to improve on things. Setting appropriate (SMART) goals and focusing on things you can control will help to break the vicious circle.

6. False permanence

Favourite saying: 'Things will never get better.'

Are you guilty of thinking that a negative situation will always stay exactly as it is? Are you convinced that you'll never live down a mistake you made or that you'll never get over that one terrible show? Then you're guilty of attaching false permanence to things. But whether we like it or not, time does tend to 'heal all wounds'. Convincing yourself that things will never change also means you're effectively denying yourself the chance to improve on things. You're declaring yourself helpless by attaching far too much importance on one single event. Much better to focus on how to shape a future you like.

7. Over-generalising or labelling

Favourite saying: 'I've come last at my last show. I'm such a loser. I always lose.'

Here we go again. Developing broad-scale categories on the basis of one example. Yes, it might be easy to do it like that, but it's far from accurate. After all, can you really determine patterns on the basis of one or a few examples? Of course you can't. The problem though is that if you regularly use words like 'always', 'never', all the time or come up with negative labels such as 'loser' or 'idiot' you will eventually start to believe in them. After a while, you'll end up behaving accordingly. Best to stay away from making any general comments, and assess each situation on its individual merit.

8.   Magical thinking

Favourite saying: 'If I only had more money, I'd be a brilliant rider.'

Welcome to Fantasyland! If only you had a fairy godmother, who would grant you every wish, then you'd be happy. True? False! Unfortunately, most of the problems we experience are not solved by the stroke of a magic wand – and only very few by a wad of cash. That's because the solution to any problem usually lies within you. While an external source might perhaps be able to ease the strain for a little while, there's no way it can fix everything all of the time. You have to do that all by yourself. So you might as well stop waiting for that knight in shining armour and pick up the sword yourself.

9.   Catastrophising

Favourite saying: 'If I don't do well at the next show, my world will collapse around me.'

Making things in your past, present or future out to be worse than they really are falls under the heading of catastrophising – also commonly known as making 'mountains out of molehills'. We tend to use this strategy because we're trying to avoid doing something or to get a little bit of sympathy from those around us. The tricky bit? It often works, too. You successfully convince yourself that whatever you're facing is so terrible, you'd be crazy to even try it. So you don't, thus reinforcing the initial notion that, really, it was too terrible. At the same time, those around you dutifully feel sorry for you, empathise and generally cause a whole lot of fuss for your sake (well, they're your friends, after all), once again making you think that you did well to over-dramatise. But if you dare to put things in perspective, tackle whatever it is you're so worried about, you'll generally realise that, actually, it wasn't all that bad.

10. Emotional reasoning

Favourite saying: 'I can't motivate myself, so it mustn't be very exciting/ worthwhile/useful.'

Yes, your emotions are important. Yes, they provide an important parameter for what a situation might mean to you. But they aren't facts. Nor should you act as if they were. Emotions are a reaction to situations based on previous experiences, personality and your current state of mental and physical well-being. Thus, your emotions can never be an objective parameter of any situation. Nor should they be. Much better to give yourself a little time and distance and then reanalyse the situation at hand. Most of the time, you'll find that your preferred course of action will change too.

11. Mind-reading (jumping to conclusions)

Favourite saying: 'That judge has given me a poor score because he/she hates me (and/or my horse).'

Sometimes we all pretend we're experts at what other people are thinking, why they're thinking it and what they will do as a result. And because we already know, we'll act accordingly. Better to be on the offensive than on the defensive. Right?

So you end up doing – or not doing – things, because you think you already know the outcome or how other people might react. You refuse to compete at a particular show, because you know who's judging – and that judge doesn't like you anyway. Or you avoid speaking to one of the girls at the yard, because you're convinced she hates you. After all, she sniped at you the other day.

But what if that particular judge really quite likes your horse, but simply didn't think you rode well enough? Or the girl at the yard had simply had a terrible day at work and felt guilty that she'd been mean?

Trying to read minds is a dangerous business, not only because it can make you feel bad, but because it can also try perfectly good relationships.

So next time, when you're inclined to jump to conclusions, how about asking that judge for some tips on how to score better the next time?

12. Double standards

Favourite saying: 'I tell my friend that of course it's normal if her horse doesn't perform well every single day. But not my horse, he doesn't do off-days.'

Does this ring a bell? Other people can make mistakes. After all they're human. But you? No, you can't possibly. It's what's called applying double standards and it harks back to wanting to be perfect all of the time – with the only difference that you don't expect anyone else to be. So who says you have to be any different? Who says you should even try? Allowing yourself the kind of slack you permit your friends will allow you to relax once in a while. And it might have the added benefit that your friends won't think you consider yourself better than they are…

13. Fallacy of fairness

Favourite saying: 'But it's not fair.'

Err… Who says life is fair? It might sound harsh, but unfortunately life, and in particular horsey life, isn't always fair. If you don't believe it, read through some of the stories in chapter 3. The true test of life is not how fair it is but how you deal with the difficult situations that come your way. And that, as we've learned, is all about staying mentally tough.

And? Did any of this sound familiar?

Never fear. It's perfectly normal. Even though it's not constructive, it's perfectly normal to think like this once in a while. The key is to recognise it and, most importantly, do something about it[73] …

This is where cognitive restructuring comes in. As the name suggests,

---

73   While it is perfectly normal to think like this some of the time, if you find yourself thinking like this most of the time or even all of the time, you should go and talk to your GP or a psychology professional

the technique revolves around restructuring negative thought patterns into more constructive, positive and – in the context of this book – effective self-talk.

Imagine finding yourself in a similar situation to Viktor. You're at an important competition. There're lots of people watching who you'd really quite like to impress – or who've done a lot to help you get this far. Then, suddenly, out of the blue, something happens. Something unfortunate, something you might or might not have been able to foresee.

Your horse loses a shoe. The zip of your boot breaks. You've left your bridle hanging in your tack room at home. Now what?

Your first reaction is likely to be feeling overwhelmed and unable to cope. In stressful situations we are prone to fall back into standard patterns of behaviour (which, incidentally, is the reason why you should practise all these mental skills in training at home so they become second nature at a show!)

So if you are inclined to engage in unproductive, dysfunctional thought patterns, such as: 'Why does this always happen to me? I'm such a klutz.' (over-generalising and labelling) or 'This is such a disaster. How can I be expected to perform like this?' (catastrophising) or 'If I could just afford better kit, farrier, horse, etc. this would never have happened' (magical thinking), you need to take action now!

1. Breathe deeply (and into your abdomen)

Just before you ask, yes, deep breathing pretty much always works! Remember, it helps to centre you, and stops or blocks out any further unwanted thoughts. It'll also slow down the physical stress response you might be experiencing. If you remember, in times of stress, our breathing rate accelerates, and we'll tend to breathe into our chest cavity. Reversing this reaction, and breathing into your belly instead will fool your body into thinking that the stressor isn't all that severe.

2. Recognise the mood state you're in

You might not be able to do something about it right at that moment (that bit comes later, once you've dealt with the crisis), but recognising what is going on, and how your thoughts affect you will at least give you some feeling of control. What is more, if you know what your ideal performance mood state is supposed to be, you'll know that you might have to take additional action later on (e.g. by using self-talk or music to get you back into the right mood state).

3. Identify the real issue at hand

So even though your first instinct might have been to think in terms of 'life's not fair' or similar, there's also a real issue at stake here – not merely your distorted version of it. Think logically. What's the problem? How does it affect your performance? Is there a viable alternative? Ask the organisers if you're allowed to start a little later, or swap starting places with another competitor; get the on-site farrier to nail the shoe back on or, if it's a soft surface and your horse doesn't get footsore, simply compete without; borrow a bridle from someone else; use a sticky bandage to hold the boot up (been there, done it!).

4. Take action

Once you've decided what you should do, don't hang about. Do it! And then go and do your thing!

TROUBLE SHOOTING

She was considered a shoe-in for winning all three classes at possibly the most prestigious international dressage competition in the world, the CHIO Aachen in 2014. After all, for two years now, Charlotte Dujardin and her wonder horse had proven themselves time and again undisputed champions of the dressage scene. As she cantered down the centre line to commence the Grand Prix, it looked like she would nail the test once again. And then… it all came crashing down around her. Mistake after mistake. First in the two-time changes, then in the tempis, followed by the pirouettes. Their final score was a far cry from the lofty percentages of competitions past, resulting in a mere sixth place. You could almost have heard the entire stadium thinking one unanimous thought. 'Now what?'

Would Charlotte manage to recover in time for the Special and the Freestyle? Or would those mistakes haunt her from now until, perhaps not all eternity, but at least for some time?

Making mistakes in competition – it's possibly one of the biggest issues for riders. We've discussed what to do right as it happens (see the previous chapter). But what about after? When you're on your way home and you know that one mistake cost you a win or a placing?

Even though we hate to acknowledge it, making mistakes is part of the game. (If you have trouble accepting that you can make a mistake, you might be prone to dysfunctional thought patterns…)

After all, making mistakes is an indication that you have tried to go the extra mile, that you dared to do something special, that something happened that is unusual. It means you've pushed your boundaries as a competitor.

But most importantly, how you deal with the mistake says a lot more about you than the mistake itself.

Charlotte showed what an outstanding rider she really is. In a message she posted on Facebook that same day she explained that, to her, it was all about getting back up and trying again.

So she did. And won the Freestyle two days later.

So how do you go about effectively dealing with mistakes?

1. 'Frame' them appropriately

Try and view your errors as a temporary glitch that can be fixed in future – not as a permanent catastrophe.

2. Check your assumptions

Do you really expect to perform faultlessly all of the time? If you do, it might make you afraid of making mistakes, thus playing it safe all of the time. But if you play it safe (trying not to make a mistake), you won't ever improve…

3. Just put it behind you

Manage your mistakes by putting them behind you when you're in the middle of a test, a course, etc. Focus on what you're doing right now (give yourself positive instructions). Once you're done, try and learn from those mistakes: what did you do, how did it happen, what can you do better next time?

4. The big picture

Don't lose sight of it! You might have a made a mistake, but there would have been a lot of things you did well too. Try and focus on those instead.

CHAPTER 11

VISUALISATION: SEEING IS BELIEVING

When a young Tim Stockdale crept out of bed late one evening to watch Mike Saywell and his horse Chainbridge winning the 1976 King George V Gold Cup, it shaped his future forever.

> 'It made such a lasting impression on me that every morning when I rode, I'd imagine myself at The Royal International with David Vine doing the commentary and introducing me to the millions of enthusiasts who were obviously watching me on TV.
>
> > "And Tim Stockdale has just cleared the combination to the King George V Gold Cup" could hear David saying in my head.
>
> > I'd canter Corky (Tim Stockdale's quirky little pony from the time he was 12) along the grass verge, humming the distinctive theme tune, imagining what it must be like to ride in front of a crowd cheering you on to victory.' [74]

Then, after 34 years, Tim's childhood dreams became reality when he won the Cup in 2010.

The power of imagery. Visualising your own perfect future – and then doing all you can to make it happen.

It's a skill that most of us will use consciously or unconsciously at some point or other during our daily activities. You might, for example,

---

74   Stockdale, T. (2012), *There's No Such Word as Can't!* Croydon, Tim Stockdale

picture how a meeting, a telephone call or an interview might go. You'll think of things you could say and try to predict how the other might respond. You'll run through as many of the options you can think of trying to make yourself appear in the best possible light.

Or on your way home at the end of a long day at work, you'll anticipate yourself lighting the barbecue, or stretching out on the sofa in front of the telly, or going for a relaxing run under the setting sun.

It works retrospectively too.

How many times haven't you played and replayed a successful show jumping round, a winning dressage test, or an exhilarating gallop across country?

Mental imagery. The ability to create or recreate an experience in the mind.

A skill that most, if not all, top athletes will consciously and deliberately use at some point or another in their career in order to improve their performance. They might use imagery to practise particular skills, a sequence of movements or to correct errors in their technique. They might use it to motivate themselves, get themselves in the right mood, or familiarise themselves with a particular setting.

The best bit?

It really works too.

Countless studies have shown that the correct and consistent practice of imagery will result in significant performance improvement.

The reason?

Put simply the brain cannot tell the difference between an actual and a vividly imagined event, meaning that the body will respond in very similar ways.

If you find this hard to believe, think of a particularly scary nightmare. Did you wake up drenched in sweat, perhaps even screaming, shaking or crying? Were you not convinced, just for a moment, that whatever had been happening in your dream, was waiting for you right here, in real life, too?

Yes? There you go then.

Even though the experience merely occurred in your mind, you still experienced it as if it was real.

Incidentally, and this is an important distinction to make, mental rehearsal or mental practice, e.g. imagining yourself repeating specific actions, techniques or skills, has been shown to be most effective. The 'daydreaming' variation of imagery, e.g. whereby you imagine outcomes, such as winning the Olympic Games, has less of an effect on tangible performance parameters. Still, the motivational and self-confidence inducing properties of simply engaging in the 'One day I will…' type of mind games should never be underestimated. Lest we forget – more often than not it starts with a dream…

A LITTLE BIT OF THEORY

But how, I hear you ask, does it work?

An excellent question. One that sport psychologists have been asking themselves for some time now. Even though we know for sure that imagery works, we're still not entirely sure as to how it does.

There are different theories relating to how the brain might actually be able to perceive the images in the first place. The so-called 'pictorialists' argue that, when engaging in imagery, the brain is in fact scanning an image that has formed in our mind. The opposite camp, the 'descriptionists' are convinced that it's not about real images, but that the language we use to describe an image makes it come to life.

Whether we believe the pictorialists or the descriptionists, it still doesn't explain why practising something in your mind improves actual performance.

Symbolic Learning Theory posits that imagery works because an athlete (rider) develops a definite plan of action. Process goals, relevant skills, alternative solutions – they're all considered in advance of execution. So when it comes to doing the real thing, it's as if you've developed a blueprint in your head. All you now need to do is follow it.

Still, Symbolic Learning Theory doesn't necessarily explain how people actually get better at skill-related tasks. If all you did was imagine how to execute a previously designed plan of action, you'd only perform within the limits of your current level. But both research and anecdotal evidence have shown that athletes who are unable to practise due to injury still manage to maintain their levels of skill. And even though actual practice still tops imagery in terms of skill development, the combination of the two has seen athletes make quite astounding progress.

This is where Psychoneuro-muscular Theory comes in, suggesting that when we imagine performing an activity, the same neuro-muscular patterns are activated as when we're engaging in the activity for real – only that they'd be lower in intensity. What this means is that even though a particular muscle might not actually be moving, subliminal commands are nevertheless sent from the brain (they're just not quite strong enough to elicit movement) – so muscles are able to practise.

So has this been proven? Sort of.

So far, a number of studies have been able to show that whenever athletes engage in imagery, their otherwise inactive muscles show subliminal electrical activity. Even though we don't yet know whether this is the exact same kind of electrical activity as during the real movement, chances are, that when visualising an activity or task, the brain develops relevant motor schemata.

In all likelihood, the benefits of imagery combine Symbolic Learning Theory with Psychoneuro-muscular Theory.

This harks back to what we've discussed during previous chapters. In order to perform optimally you must know what to do. And imagery is all about knowing precisely what to do. If you have a clear picture in your mind of what you're about to do next, you'll have a clear goal, you'll know the specific skills you'll need, and you'll know how it should all feel (see below). In addition, effectively showing your brain what a particular skill looks and feels like, you'll be clearing a path for any future motor commands.

A MATTER OF PERSPECTIVE

But regardless of which explanation holds true, the fact is, it works. If done correctly, that is. Let's take a look at some of the preconditions of getting your imagery just right.

First of all, there are two perspectives from which to view yourself. Either internally, as if you were actually right there, on your horse, riding, able to see your hands, your horse's neck and mane, his ears moving this way and that.

Or you might view yourself from an external perspective, as if you were a coach, a judge or an onlooker. You'll be able to see what you and your horse look like when you're performing any given movement, the shape your horse makes over a fence, whether your horse's nose is on the vertical, behind or above it.

Neither perspective is intrinsically better than the other – or rather, both have their advantages and disadvantages.

First off, an internal perspective probably feels more natural to you. After all, you'll see things that you usually see when you're sitting in the saddle. Especially when you're first starting out with an imagery programme you might be inclined to use an internal perspective, because, well, it's easier. And you know what? That's fine. Especially when trying to get to grips with some tricky skills or movements.

But there might come a time when you might want to 'polish' the overall picture, before a dressage show for example. Or you might want to correct an error in positioning or outline, that you know is there, but you can't quite get a handle on. Using an external perspective can work wonders, simply because it is more difficult. Remember, challenging yourself improves performance…

ALL THOSE SENSES

Imagery. It's all about seeing yourself perform, right?

Wrong. Or at least, not quite right.

Remember the descriptionists' explanation for why imagery works? It is our language that makes an experience come to life. But words don't merely paint a picture. They also describe how something might sound, smell or taste. Most importantly though, the words used during imagery should describe how an experience might feel.

What does it feel like as your horse engages his hind quarters? What does it feel like when he is soft in the contact? What do 'keeping a rhythm' or 'collection' feel like?

In all likelihood, as you read these words, the physical sensation of your horse moving underneath will come rushing into, well, your head, your mind, but also your body. So despite the name, imagery isn't merely about images. It's just as much about the feeling you have as you execute whatever it is you're visualising. In sport psychology circles, this is also called kinaesthetic imagery.

If you really want to make an experience as real and life-like as possible, you mustn't forget about sound, smell or (if the situation warrants it) taste. It is those sensory experiences that create (or recreate) the all-important context. If you are trying to create a realistic blueprint of a situation, that allows your mind and body to act accordingly, the 'trappings' of a show or any other important event are almost as important as going into the ring. In fact, a lot of the time, it's precisely those trappings that make your nervous or unsure.

Worried whether you'll be able to handle all those spectators? Include them in your visualisation. Watch and listen as they clap and cheer you on.

Not sure what to do when you're halting in front of the judges' box? Visualise it. Watch his or her face break into a smile or observe as his or her features remain carefully neutral.

Need a bit more detail to make sure you've got the atmosphere down to a T? Imagine the smell of the obligatory burger-and-chip van.

Creating or recreating an experience is therefore (almost) as much about hearing, smelling and tasting as it is about seeing and feeling. Incidentally, it doesn't matter whether you are visualising from an internal or external perspective – the use of all the senses should remain the same.

By now you should have a relatively clear idea about what imagery actually is. Which means that it's time to take a look at when you might want to use it.

Allan Urho Paivio, Emeritus Professor of Psychology at the University of Western Ontario, was the first to clarify that imagery has, in fact, both a cognitive and a motivational function. In his theory, somewhat unimaginatively called the Two-Dimensional Model, he argued that different imagery types could be divided into different functions and applications. The cognitive function of imagery is used to develop sport-specific skills and plan appropriate strategies in advance of competition. The motivational function on the other hand relates to how imagery might be used to picture, and ultimately reach your goals, cope effectively when things get tough, and help you achieve your optimal level of arousal. In fact, arousal control came to be seen as an altogether separate function of imagery. As a result, the motivational dimension of Paivio's Two-Dimensional Model ended up being separated into mastery and arousal – effectively replacing the original 2 x 2 model with a 3 x 2 model…

Because in addition to the purpose (e.g. mastery or arousal), imagery might also be applied to different situations (the application dimension). They might either be very specific and relate to one particular skill or event. Or they might be rather general and describe how you feel or behave in a more generic sporting context.

So let's explore them one by one and see how they might be applied.

Cognitive Specific – improve your skills

This type of imagery is all about a specific skill and visualising (e.g. using all the senses) yourself executing it appropriately. Incidentally, this also includes error correction or when you can't train for real due to injury (yours or your horse's). Imagine yourself riding a movement in dressage or approaching and jumping a fence in the desired way. Visualise how you apply the relevant aids, your seat, your legs, your hands, and feel how your horse responds to them. See the letter you are aiming for and feel yourself ride the line towards it. Imagine how you collect your horse a few strides out from the fence and how, subsequently, the horse takes you forward and over it.

Cognitive General – plan ahead

Cognitive General imagery revolves around visualising general strategies you might adopt throughout the course of a competition, such as how you might ride a cross-country course or endurance event. What kind of rhythm or tempo are you aiming for? What kind of outline should you ride your horse in? How are you planning to react to changes of direction, or what will you do when other riders overtake you? It's what Pippa Funnell did on the morning of the cross-country at the 2000 Sydney Olympics.

'So I found a corner in the stable canteen for a quiet coffee, and mentally rode the course fence by fence in a positive way.'

Motivational Specific – arousal – emotional control

As you know, optimal performance depends quite a bit on the right feel of your body. Are you sufficiently relaxed, yet alert enough to nail that last fence, that last salute? Imagery can help you visualise precisely how you should feel, physically and emotionally and what you need to do just before you're going to execute that particular movement. That's what is called emotional control. Perhaps you need to use a trigger word, or take a single deep breath. Whatever it may be, visualise yourself using the right kind of strategies to get you into that perfect state of arousal. So really, this type of imagery can serve as a reminder, as a cue, and, as we've already discussed, as a blueprint for your actual performance.

Motivational General – arousal – managing competitive anxiety

What's your personal 'oomph' score? How many butterflies do you need zooming round your belly in order to feel at your best? Use imagery to visualise yourself getting into the right state of arousal before every competition and it can be a great asset to combat any competitive anxiety you might feel. Use it as part of your pre-competitive routine (see the following chapter) and before you tackle any skill-related imagery.

Motivational Specific – mastery – improve your confidence

See yourself in a specific situation that is highly motivating, and shows you 'mastering' it (thus the name Motivational Specific – mastery). You might see yourself clear the last fence (something that is notoriously tricky to do, as, quite often, riders are so 'relieved' that they're almost home safely, they lose focus just prior to that last fence). Or you might see yourself nail that last salute, and subsequently see yourself punch the air with joy, then gratefully scratch your horse's withers. Use your own positive experience from a show or a training session to provide yourself with some extra inspiration.

Motivational General – mastery – confidence, commitment, control

When using this type of imagery, you should visualise yourself performing as if no task is too difficult. You'll see yourself fully focused, in control, and succeeding at whatever you set your mind to. Your images are positive and you're the one in control. Once again, if you're in need of a confidence boost, simply visualise a previously successful event. Quite simply, it's as if you're watching a major action movie, and you're the hero that saves the day. All by him/herself.

It's what Mary King does, too.

'If I am hacking along, thinking about a big event in the next few days, I'll be imagining galloping round the cross country course and coming inside, and finishing in-time. I always have these positive thoughts, I never think: "Oh, I might fall off" or anything. I might, but I don't think about that. I think of galloping and doing well. I think that's the key thing, to be positive in my thoughts about the upcoming event.'

As with most things, using imagery – and doing it well – requires practice. That's because controlling your images isn't always easy. Sometimes they tend to start living a life of their own, and you might end up seeing yourself doing just what you were trying to avoid. (As always, whenever we're worried, we tend to focus on just the situation that scares us just that little bit.) Never fear though, controllability can be practised. So can vividness and the involvement of all your senses. If you're only just starting out with imagery, you might therefore go with Imagery Training Programme 1, as outlined below. If you think you've got sufficient control over your images, and can create them as life-like as possible, you might consider Imagery Training Programme 2.

Most importantly though, whether you're just starting out or consider yourself an expert, imagery is performed best when you're relaxed – thus counteracting any anxiety-related shifts of focus.

MENTAL IMAGERY PROGRAMME 1 (MIP1) (NOVICE)

1. Hide away

To begin, find yourself a quiet corner where you're unlikely to be disturbed. Make yourself comfortable. You're going to be sitting or lying like that for some time, so best not twist any limbs.

2. Relax

Breathe deeply and into your abdomen. Remember, when you breathe in, your tummy should inflate, like a balloon. When you exhale, it should deflate, contracting into the direction of your spine. You might want to try breathing out twice as long as you breathe in, and opening your lips slightly as you breathe out. Repeat a few times, until you're nice and relaxed. If you've been practising deep breathing in combination with a trigger word, now's the time to use that too.

3. Easy does it

Some people suggest visualising circles that grow larger and smaller, filling them with colour. This is to help you gain control of your images, including their vividness. If, however, you find this too tedious and can only bear to do it once or twice, you might move on to simple, emotionally neutral scenarios. Again, the emphasis here is on practising control of your images. If you jump straight in with something you've been desperately trying to improve in training, and that's been worrying you at some level, you're likely to keep seeing yourself doing things wrong – and that is something you want to try to avoid! So, stick with the easy stuff. How about visualising yourself sweeping the yard or cleaning tack? Include as many sensory details as possible. Visualise yourself coughing as you breathe in the dust or breathe in deeply as the distinct smell of saddle soap enters your nostrils.

4. It's in the detail

As you gain confidence, continue to include additional elements. A horse snorting in his stable. The yard cat purring as you scratch him. You might even advance to brushing and tacking up your horse (unless, of course, that's a major source of distress). Include aspects such as that unforgettable horsey smell, the way his coat feels as you stroke his neck, the sound his hooves make as you lead him from the box.

5. One more time: relax!

At the end of your session, make sure you breathe in deeply several more times. You want your body to learn that visualisation is a pleasant, relaxing experience, rather than something to get worked up about! When you open your eyes, take your time coming to. Don't just spring into action straight away or many of the relaxing associations will be lost.

Practise this initial programme regularly (preferably every day, for example as you're about to go to sleep), and you'll find that you'll gain increasing control over your images. While virtually impossible to set an exact time frame – everyone does imagery at their own pace – you'll know when you're ready to move on to the next programme. You'll have no problems focusing on the sensations (e.g. pictures plus other sensory experiences) and they'll follow your script (rather than lead a life of their own.)

So, once you're there, time to move on to....

MENTAL IMAGERY PROGRAMME 2 (MIP2) (ADVANCED)

1. Relax

Right, no more hiding away for MIP2. The reason? You'll need to practise visualising wherever, whenever. After all, you'll want to be able to use it in a competitive environment, and you might not be able to find anywhere nice and quiet. Still, in the beginning, or if you've got a longer mental practice session planned, try and find somewhere where you won't be disturbed every couple of minutes. But whatever your location, you must be able to relax before you start. The reasons behind this are exactly the same as in MIP1 – you don't want to start associating imagery with stress. This means that you should start each session with several deep breaths, preferably accompanied with your chosen trigger word.

2.   Know what you want

Here we go again. It boils down to the same thing, doesn't it? Make sure you know what you want to achieve and how you're going to go about it. In imagery terms this means you should be clear

A   whether you want to practise a skill or technical element (cognitive imagery), work on your perception of achievement (motivational imagery – mastery) or getting yourself into the right zone (motivational imagery – arousal), and,

B   whether you want to run through a specific situation, such as a movement or fence, or something more general, such as your preparation before an event.

3.   Picture the scene

Know what you want? Good. Start by visualising the accompanying scene as vividly as possible. There should be as much detail as you can think of. Remember, the most effective imagery is as life-like as possible, so the more real you make your scene, the better it'll work.

4.   Practise, practise, practise

As you visualise yourself performing, regardless of whether you are using an internal or external perspective, make sure you involve all your senses, including feel (kinaesthetic imagery). Start off slowly and deliberately, going through your movements step by step. Especially if you're working on error correction, make sure you don't rush through the movements. Then, as you gain in confidence, speed up the pace until you're performing in real time. This'll take quite some concentrating, but it'll get easier with, you guessed it, practise. (If you're finding it tough to keep a hold on all the different images, check out the trouble shooting section below for some tips to help you.)

5. Your routine

You know by now: 'routines rock!' Routines that incorporate imagery are no different. In fact, they can work wonders (once you've achieved good control over your images that is. Remember, whatever you visualise must be positive!). A routine that includes imagery will ensure that you have the most definite of all plans, as you'll have seen yourself perform before you're actually going out there to do it for real. So any such routine might look something like this: (1) breathe, (2) centre yourself, (3) trigger word (either to reduce arousal or to guide your focus), (4) a short 'clip' of yourself performing as you want to perform, (5) give the aid to enter the ring/come out of the starting box/etc.

So then, working through a programme such as MIP2 will develop your imagery skills in such a way that you should be able to incorporate them prior to each performance. What is more, imagery will also increase your ability to focus, help you overcome pre-competition nerves and get you in your optimal state of arousal. Even if you've only got one horse to ride, or are out of action due to injury, imagery will ensure you don't lose 'it'.

The only thing you have to do in return? Stick to the rules and keep up the good work.

TROUBLE SHOOTING

First things first. Some people are naturally born visualisers. They just tend to find it easy. Other people find it harder. It's normal and just another example of 'individual differences'. But that doesn't mean to say that imagery can't be beneficial even to someone who struggles with it in the beginning.

You'll be relieved to hear that there are several means to help you become more confident and more adept at visualising relevant sport-specific skills.

1.   Write out a script

We've already used the movie analogy, so let's just take it one step further. Imagine you're a writer developing a new script. It's a blockbuster about a dressage rider/show jumper/eventer/endurance rider/vaulter who's about to achieve a personal best/master a particular skill/ overcome his/her fears/ etc. And you are the main cast! All you need to do is write down what exactly you're planning to do and when. Include references to how you might feel from a biomechanical, physical or psychological perspective. Don't forget to describe the setting and be as detailed as you can. As you write, the images will come to you. Remember the pictorialists' explanation of imagery – well, you're simply taking the whole process and putting it on paper. Once you've completed your script, read it through, and really feel yourself becoming engrossed in the situation. After a while, you'll be able to visualise without the script too.

2.   Sketch it

Not much of a writer? Never fear! You can just draw how you're planning to ride. The obvious downside is that you'll be foregoing some of the details, but as you draw, you'll develop a good sense of what you should be doing – which is, of course, the essence of good imagery.

3.   Watch it

Missing some inspiration on where or how to start with your imagery? How about watching an inspiring video, either of yourself as you perform really well, or of a rider you admire. Then use that as, for lack of a better expression, a blueprint for your mental blueprint. Beware though that if you're watching a top rider, you should know what it is they are doing, otherwise you'll struggle to develop the correct neural pathways for relevant muscle activity.

But what if, after all that, things still go wrong? Say you've always relied on a blueprint of yourself performing well in competition for your imagery. It's worked brilliantly in the past, too. But, then, two weeks back, you had a bad fall (or a similarly unfortunate mishap) at an event. Since then, every time you try to visualise, you see yourself making a hash of things.

What now?

Making a serious mistake might well have dented your confidence. Ask yourself whether you've still got sufficient control over the images that are running through your head. To check, run through MIP1. If you're encountering problems there, try and reassert control. Run through the basic exercises until things have returned to normal.

If you find that it really is that mishap in competition that's preventing you from visualising effectively, use a positive experience in training as an imagery blueprint instead. Remember, it shouldn't matter where you perform the necessary skills, whether in training or in competition, as long as you perform them well.

Combine it with some of the tips relating to goal-setting, self-talk, and a relevant routine, and you should be able to get a grip on your problem in no time.

And most importantly – forgive yourself that mistake…

Reframe it and just put it behind you.

PART III

PREPARING FOR COMPETITION

CHAPTER 12

START OF THE SEASON: PLANNING + PREPARATION = PERFORMANCE

The achievement of the British 'Golden Trio' at the 2012 London Olympics was, quite simply, nothing short of amazing. In one hundred years of dressage at the Olympics the Brits had never before won a medal. Not of any colour, let alone gold, either in the team or in the individual event.

But the team of Carl Hester with Uthopia, Laura Bechtolsheimer (now Tomlison) with Mistral Hojris and Charlotte Dujardin with Valegro changed all that!

While the press heralded the performance in London's Greenwich Park as something close to magical, most of us who ride horses know that nothing could be further from the truth.

No magic, just incredibly hard work. And dedication. And planning. Lots and lots of planning.

When Charlotte Dujardin and Valegro won the British Championships at Prix St. George level in 2010, Carl Hester reportedly told the press that this wouldn't be the end, but that the 2012 Olympics were the final goal.[75] That same year, the British quartet of Laura Bechtolsheimer, Fiona Bigwood, Carl Hester and Maria Eilberg rode their way to a team silver, and Laura Bechtolsheimer topped off the experience with an individual silver at the 2010 World Equestrian Games in Kentucky – making dressage aficionados sit up and take notice of the British potential blossoming at the edge of the horizon.

---

75   Hester, C. (2014), *Making it Happen*, London, Orion Books

By 2011, it had become crystal clear that the Brits had turned into a force – no, a tornado – to be reckoned with. At the European Championships in Rotterdam that same year, the future Golden Trio plus Emile Faurie on Elmegardens Marquis took Team Gold, with Carl Hester earning individual silver on the stunning Uthopia and Laura Becholtsheimer individual bronze on her trusted partner Mistral Horjis. In her first (!) season at Grand Prix level, Charlotte ended up sixth on Valegro (who else?).

It was the boost the team needed in the year before an Olympics. And it was a premeditated boost, carefully orchestrated to give all three riders the best chance to peak when it mattered most – at the Olympic Games.

REACHING THE TOP... AT THE RIGHT TIME

Peaking

It's a concept more commonly known from sports such as athletics, swimming or cycling. In preparation for a major event, athletes 'pace' themselves to make sure that, come the big day, they are at their optimum fitness, but not hampered by the tiredness or staleness that goes along with training for too hard or too long.

Unfortunately, to this day, many athletes, including riders, seem to be proponents of the 'more is better' philosophy. Combined with ego-orientations and certain dysfunctional thought patterns (along the lines of 'I must win all the time'), 'more equals better' will almost inevitably lead to 'more equals complete breakdown'.

What is more, expecting to be able to perform at your absolute maximum all of the time, from the beginning of the season right through until the end, will not only wear out your horse, it will eventually lead to you feeling frustrated, disheartened and unwilling to keep going.

I know what you're thinking.

You're thinking that setting ambitious, challenging goals, and training for them with all the determination and commitment you can muster is fundamental in order to reach your dreams.

You're right, of course.

In order to improve performance, body and mind need to be pushed beyond their current limits. In order to achieve ever greater heights, you need to be ambitious in what you set out to do. It's called the principle of 'progressive overload' and describes how body (and mind) should be pushed beyond its limits time and again, in order to adapt and improve. Yet progressive overload must not be taken too far, lest body (or mind) break down. Then, performance will stagnate or decrease. Progressively overloading body (or mind) only improves performance as long as you give either system the chance to make the necessary adjustments (an increase in muscle mass or lung volume, for example, or in developing the necessary mental skills). If you keep pushing at a rate that is faster and harder than body (or mind) can cope with, you'll risk breakdown.

Confusing? Oh yes.

It all boils down to this: in order to reach your ultimate performance, you need to find the precarious balance between training and relaxation, for yourself, your horse, at a physical and mental level.[76]

And yet… it can be so tempting, can't it?

Does the following scenario sound familiar?

Things have been going so well, these last few weeks. You're desperate to keep it that way, so you keep training and training and training. The day before the show arrives. You could really do with another confidence boost before tomorrow, so you'll get in another good, solid training session – even though you've already trained really hard all week.

But rather than improving, your horse seems to be getting more obstinate by the day. He refuses to be 'through', isn't as responsive to the leg nor as soft in the mouth. So you train some more, in the hope you might crack it in time.

But the competitive performance on the day of the show leaves much to be desired.

---

76 While the scope of this book is almost exclusively focused on the mental components of the rider, a point of notice seems to be in order. Despite considerable advances in recognising both the physiological and psychological markers of overtraining, too many horses are regularly pushed beyond what they can cope with – both physically and psychologically. Adopting a plan of periodisation will ensure not only peak performances but can also help to safeguard the well-being of our four-legged partner.

Surprised? Probably not!

So how do you train without *over*training?

This is where the concept of periodisation comes in. Even though *Perfect Mind: Perfect Ride* is not (nor is it meant to be) a book on physiology, the concept is of value also from a sport psychological point of view.

Varying training components throughout any particular competitive cycle, athletes (humans and equines alike) are able to maintain and improve sporting performance while minimising training problems such as staleness, overtraining, burnout or injury. The key components we're talking about are 'training volume' and 'training intensity'. Training volume is essentially a measure of the amount of training athletes perform, while training intensity refers to the quality of the training. In simple terms, training can be high volume and low intensity (long hacks at a walk or a slow trot, for example), low volume and high intensity (such as quick bursts of effort, such as several minutes of highly collected work, or jumping efforts), or high volume and high intensity (galloping for long periods of time). You will have gathered by now that too much high volume, high intensity work, especially prior to competition is tempting fate as it can increase the likelihood for sustaining an injury, causing staleness or overtraining...

So then, how to overcome that fallacy of thought that 'more and more' equals 'better and better'?

In addition to the long-, medium-, and short-term goals we've already discussed, training can also be divided into

1. Long-term training cycles (macrocycles)

These usually vary in duration from several months (e.g. a competitive season culminating in the regional or national championships) to several years (e.g. the four years between Olympic Games, or the two years between a World Championship and Olympic Games).

2. Medium-term training cycles (mesocycles)

Each macrocycle is split into several mesocycles, ranging from several weeks to a year in duration, with an important event at the end of each cycle. If your macrocycle constituted an Olympic quadrennial, your mesocycles will probably culminate in a European Championship (end of mesocycle 1), a World Championship (end of mesocycle 2) and, again a European Championship (end of mesocycle 3). The last, fourth, mesocycle, would end with the Olympic Games. If your macrocycle culminated with a National Championship, your mesocycles would focus on qualifying competitions.

3. Short-term training microcycles, or 'phases'

Each mesocycle is once again split into four distinct training phases: preparatory, competitive, peaking and recovery. Each preparatory phase occurs at the start of a season or mesocycle and aims to prepare you and your horse both physically and mentally for what lies ahead. As the name suggests, the competitive phase focuses on you being able to perform consistently in competition, culminating in top performances in the third phase, the peaking phase (that's when the main event at the end of the mesocycle takes place, such as a championship). Most importantly, any peaking phase must be followed by a recovery phase to make sure both of you are able to recover fully before the start of the next mesocycle.

It's important to the ultimate success of your training cycles that you look at your and your horse's individual strengths and weaknesses while planning them. If your horse struggles to carry himself, you might need to extend your preparatory phase to strengthen him sufficiently before you move into your competitive phase and end up being disappointed. If your horse is prone to injury, you might need to adjust the training workload accordingly. Adjust volume and intensity according to your horse's need and make sure you keep listening to signals of overtraining, staleness and the first inklings of injury.

CYCLES AND GOALS – STRONGER TOGETHER

So where does sport psychology come into all this?

Perhaps you've already guessed it. Remember all the talk about goals?

Those long-term, medium-term, short-term goals (they should obviously all be SMART, too)? The performance profiling I encouraged you to do? Well, here's your chance to structure them into appropriate training cycles.

Think of your long-term goal. This'll be the culmination of your macrocycle. Think of Charlotte and Carl when they figured Valegro would end up an Olympic horse. Think of the British team, that, well before the 2012 Olympics, started to have dreams of an Olympic medal.

Then think of any medium-term markers to set yourself. There you've got your mesocycles. Think Valegro's national championship win in the Prix St. George. Think of the British silver medal at the World Championships in 2010 and, one year later, at the European Championships.

That leaves your microcycles, e.g. the four phases (preparatory, competitive, peaking, recovery). Think back to the results of your performance profile and the resultant short-term, process goals. Where would you need to fit them into your different phases?

Chances are, some process goals will be constants, such as keeping your horse through and soft. They will also frequently be doubling up as trigger words to help you in your concentration or to keep your self-talk positive and constructive. Essentially, these types of process goals will be like red threads weaving their way through the preparatory, competitive and peaking phases.

Then there're elements that you should really have sorted before you're off to compete, such as particular movements. They'll belong primarily to your preparatory phase.

Finally, there's the recovery phase. I can't stress it enough: this phase is vital, and in many ways more important than all the other ones. Improvement in training only occurs if you allow sufficient time for recovery after a period of intensive training. While there can be no doubt that this is particularly important to keep your horse healthy and sound, don't underestimate the importance of giving yourself a little down time too.

We've discussed it at length – trying to be the best you can be is hard work. Being completely, utterly committed is at times utterly exhausting. So give yourself a little bit of time off. Even if you still feel the urge to ride, do it without the pressure of having to train. Do something different. You'll probably end up learning something new while you're at it too…

Bear in mind that the structured development of your mental skills should also feature in any mesocycle and the four corresponding phases, depending on how they help and support your performance.

Goal-setting, for example, should be done right at the beginning of your preparatory phase – or even during your previous recovery phase. But if you know you're prone to dysfunctional thought patterns, work on those in your preparatory phase to enable you to use self-talk most effectively in your competitive phase.

If your levels of arousal tend to spiral out of control come competition time, make sure you work on relevant relaxation techniques, including routines, now, before you're off competing regularly.

Can't seem to hold your focus? Work shifting your attention towards relevant cues, and establish a solid routine to initiate focus.

Do you end up imagining yourself getting things wrong? Spend your preparatory phase getting control of your mental images, progressively making it more challenging until you are capable of visualising a complete script of yourself performing optimally.

Planning your competitive future, your year, your season in a structured manner can also make a considerable difference to how you approach each competition. Suddenly, you'll be riding 'in context'. It's no longer merely about achieving optimal performances, but performing within the framework of a – your – bigger picture. Competing at the start of your competitive phase doesn't have to result in the same scores as in your peaking phase. Far from it. In fact, you're supposed to start off slowly and grow as you go on. Knowing this, having planned and anticipated it, will not only result in peace of mind but also in increased confidence in yourself and your horse. After all, you really know what you're doing.

Still, there's even more you can do – leading us neatly on to the next, yet related, topic.

DEAR DIARY...

Most riders are taught to focus on the present, work towards the future, and not dwell too much on the past. I wholeheartedly agree when you're in the middle of a competition. Spending precious time and mental energy worrying about what is impossible to change, has rarely done anybody any good.

However, we've also seen that top riders (and, in fact, all top athletes) make the effort to critically evaluate past events. More importantly, they do so with an exacting eye for detail.

This is exactly where your own training diary will come in handy. As you train and compete your way through the various stages, there'll be a number of factors that influence your performance. Not all of them you'll be able to control (and nor should you try). Still, mapping them, monitoring them, analysing whether and how they influence your performance can work wonders for how you plan your training.

That's how Sjef Janssen, former Dutch national trainer, husband of Anky van Grunsven – and current trainer of Matthias Alexander Rath and Totilas – thinks about it, too:

'It is exceptionally useful to record your findings during training and competitions. It'll allow you to determine certain patterns during periods when things are either going well or somewhat less so. It's also easier to determine any possible cause. The way to the top is one of endless learning and requires new insights all the time. You need to do your homework, day in, day out, and then you'll look back at things that happened. These are important moments from which to learn.' [77]

Indeed!

So why not try and optimise your training through keeping a detailed diary? Make a note of the time of day, where you rode, the surroundings, the surface, the weather. Keep a record on the type of training (i.e. volume and intensity), what you worked on, things that went well, difficulties you faced, how you solved them (if you did). Make sure you also keep a close eye on management details, such as the type and quantity of feed, when

---

77   Heuitink, J. and Schoorl, H. (2010), *Het Loboek voor de dressuur ruiter*, EiS Expertise in Sport

your horse was fed, if, when and for how long he was turned out, whether in a field or a paddock, how long you groomed him and whether he's able to socialise with other horses. At a competition, you might also want to note down your preparation routine, the specifics of your warm-up, and various elements that went well or not so well while you were actually competing.

Do this throughout a season and you'll end up with a wealth of information that you'll be able to draw on come competition time – and especially when you seem to have lost your 'mojo'.

Let's face it. It *does* happen…

Instead of continuing to improve, your performances keep getting worse. Despite all your hard work, you cannot seem to turn things around. This is where your training diary comes in handy.

Think back to the last time you performed at your very best at a show: you and your horse were relaxed, yet alert. Fully focused on the task at hand, but still able to deal effectively with anything unforeseen, such as changes in the schedule, bad weather or even getting stuck in traffic on the way there. Not surprisingly, your final score turned out to be your best ever! Now try and recall a show you'd really much rather forget; where everything that could possibly go wrong, did end up going wrong; where you and your horse were stressed, anxious and ready to snap at anyone and everything – and where the final result left a lot to be desired. Same horse–rider combination, two very different outcomes – what happened?

The question that you need to ask yourself, preferably with pen and paper at the ready, is what you did differently prior to, and during, one show compared to the other. Essentially, everything we do conforms to the principles of cause and effect, meaning that any actions we take have consequences. Most of the time, such consequences will be minor and not impact greatly on our lives. In the world of equestrian sports, however, which are ruled by the subtle interactions between horse and human, any changes in the physical and mental well-being of the rider are likely to affect the behaviour, and subsequent performance, of the horse.

Probably the most obvious aspect to consider is the daily training and management of your horse in the run up to the show. How often you trained, what you did, and how the horse responded are questions that – hopefully – should be second nature to most riders. Next, you might wish to think about the specifics regarding your own life: were you under any sort of stress (for example work- or family-related issues that you found difficult to deal with); did you have sufficient 'down time', get plenty of sleep and eat well? Lastly, try and evaluate precisely what you did upon arrival at the show ground. How much time did you have before you had to get ready and what did you do to fill it, what were the general conditions (e.g. temperature, weather, surface, etc.) and how did you structure your warm-up?

By the time you have thus compared both your 'personal best' and 'rather left unmentioned' examples of competitive outings, you should have a pretty clear idea of the kind of things that do and do not work in your and your horse's favour.

From now on, hit-and-miss preparation in the run up to a show will be a thing of the past.

RESHAPING HABITS OF A LIFETIME

By now we've considered how to structure your competitive approach, how to incorporate goal-setting into the various training cycles and how to include mental training into your competitive season.

But there's something we haven't touched on.

You. The human athlete. Because that is what you are. And it's how you should treat yourself.

Once again, this is not a book on exercise or training science. Nor is it a book on sports nutrition. Still, being the best you can be and consistently creating the perfect ride, means considering the whole package. This is often referred to as the 'holistic' approach – a concept you might have heard of in conjunction with the training of your horse. What it means is that in addition to making sure your riding and horse management is up to scratch, you also need to take into account other things that influence how you perform on the day.

Such as physical fitness, including core elements such as endurance (e.g. aerobic fitness), strength (in particular core stability), flexibility.

Or eating healthily. And, no, I don't just mean on the day before a show.

Or getting sufficient sleep. For some riders, this can be a real issue, considering their multiple commitments of riding, teaching, working, and looking after the family and the house.

Ask yourself these questions: do you notice that you're out of breath at the end of a test, a course, a competition? Are there moments in your training when you have to take a break even though, really, you should be pushing on? Do you lose your focus because you're getting tired or sore? Or perhaps because you haven't eaten all day, or not drunk enough?

Take another look at your performance profile. How did you score on the physical fitness scale? What about your eating habits or quality of sleep?

Be honest, now!

Should you – could you – be fitter or healthier?

Chances are, you'll have a pretty good idea of what you should be doing to improve your own performance in addition to riding. Like it or not, being an athlete means that you have to do additional training. You need to develop more effective habits. Easier said than done!

Whether you're a professional rider training several horses (and clients) a day, whether you hold down a job, are studying or are a full-time mum (or dad), you'll be trying to fit in your riding around all the other activities that govern your life. It seems you simply don't have the 'brain-space' to think of yet another thing you should be doing. So you postpone working out more, eating healthily, or getting more sleep until next week, next month, or, like the majority of the population, until the New Year.

Only to find that you can't stick to your new habits anyway… Frustrating doesn't even cover it!

But here's the good news. It doesn't *have* to be difficult to develop new habits.

Want to know how?

Firstly, and most importantly, you're going to have to want to change. That one's pretty obvious. If you aren't motivated to do something, you won't do it, or at least not for very long. Being autonomous and making up your own mind of how you lead your life is, after all, a fundamental human need.

Unfortunately though, most of the time motivation simply isn't enough to sustain behaviour change for any length of time.

At first glance you might find this hard to believe. And I don't blame you. After all, we've been told time again that motivation, wanting something badly enough, true and deep-felt desire are what makes the world go round (indeed, at the start of this book I've argued much the same).

And yet…

Have you ever tried to lose a habit you knew wasn't doing you any good? Such as giving up smoking, or eating too much junk food? Or you might have tried to establish a new habit instead. One that you figured might be better for your health. Such as taking up running or some other exercise regime.

Of course you have. Did you succeed? More importantly, did you succeed every time? Probably not.

Despite what people might have been telling you, the reason you didn't succeed had nothing to do with not wanting it – whatever it was – badly enough.

In fact, it had all to do with the way your brain works.

Nobel Memorial Prize winner and Professor Emeritus of Psychology and Public Affairs at Princeton University, Dr Daniel Kahneman, introduced the idea that the brain can form thoughts in two distinct ways in his best-selling book *Thinking, Fast and Slow*. There's system 1, our 'instinctive' side. Thinking is fast, automatic, emotional and subconscious. Then there's system 2. That's our 'rational' side, which comes up with thoughts in a slow, deliberate, logical, calculating and conscious way.

Whenever you first come up with an idea for a new habit, whether that's eating healthily, taking up running or integrating an imagery routine into your daily riding session, the rational part of your brain, 'system 2' calls the shots. It'll weigh up the pros and cons, try and determine the specifics, mull things over, and determine which behaviours you need to ensure your idea becomes a success. You might decide that you're going to run three days a week or that you'll try cutting down on sugar and salt by choosing healthy snacks.

Now all you need to do is integrate it into a habit that fits into your daily routine.

If you leave things to system 2, you'll struggle. More likely, you'll fail. That's because every day, you'll be trying to re-invent the wheel (figuratively speaking, of course). You'll re-evaluate the pros and cons. You'll mull things over again and again. After all, that's what your rational side does. The problem is, that, eventually, you'll probably change your mind. And nothing will come of that fantastic new habit.

Really, what you need to do is to allow system 1 to take over. System 1 is automatic and instinctive. Habits are, too. They're behaviours that have become automatic, and thus instinctive. You don't need to think about them, you just do them.

So how do you go about allowing system 1 to take over? First of all, you'll need to decide on a context-specific cue, some kind of 'external trigger' that serves as a signal to initiate your chosen behaviour, your habit. Such a trigger could be anything from seeing your running shorts lying next to your bed as you wake up in the morning, to setting your smart phone to send you a message when it's time to take your vitamin supplement.

Obviously, behaviours don't turn into habits immediately. They'll need to be initiated by the same context-specific trigger. Then they'll need to be repeated over and over, in exactly the same manner, for a number of weeks until they've become entirely automatic.

The more rewarding a particular behavioural pattern, the more quickly and easily it'll become automatic. That's why it's so important to end any new regime, such as a running session, or healthy meal, on a high. If what you're doing leaves you feeling worse than before, forming a habit will become disproportionately more difficult. The rationale behind this is simple of course: if something is pleasurable, you'll want to do it again. And again. And again.

Follow these steps and you'll turn any behavioural pattern into a habit. Then, you'll be able to keep it up indefinitely. Without having to think about it every day. And the best bit? You'll still be able to perform a deeply ingrained habit under pressure – your body will have got so used to doing just that one sequence of behaviours, it'll actually find comfort in it (that's why sport-specific routines work).

By the way, have you ever wondered what makes equestrian sports so addictive? Well, here's your answer: it's a behavioural pattern that has turned into a habit. Usually, the horse serves as the external trigger. The mere thought of him serves to initiate a whole series of behaviours that, especially if you've been riding for a few years, you don't even need to think about any more. You just do them. You'll drive to the yard, groom your horse, tack up, warm up, ride, cool down, wash your horse down, put him back in his stable or into the field.

The experience of riding is intrinsically so rewarding (usually, anyway), that you'll want to do it again. And again. As a result, the behavioural patterns repeat themselves day after day, week after week, year after year. Eventually, they'll become so ingrained you'll feel at a loss when you're not doing them – which explains why so many riders find it impossible to stay away from their horses for too long…

So let's have a look at how you'd go about developing a habit that'll help you succeed throughout the season.

1. Decide on a habit

Take a look at your performance profile. Which areas might you still need to improve on? Do you need to work on your fitness, your core stability, your flexibility? Do you need to eat more healthily or sleep better? Identify a lifestyle change you wish to pursue.

2. Choose your trigger

Look for something in your environment that you can easily associate with your behaviour. Your running shoes placed strategically where you can't overlook them as you get up in the morning? A bottle of water and glass placed next to the sink in the tack room to remind you to keep hydrated?

3. Keep the behaviour simple

Make the behavioural pattern simple enough so you can keep it going. You might now be thinking that all goals should be challenging. You'd be right. Consider this though: the fact that you are trying to establish a new, healthy habit is already a challenge in itself.

4. Choose a reward

In many ways, this links very closely to my previous point. Your new behaviour needs to be enjoyable or at least be followed by some kind of reward. Running to exhaustion if you're unfit won't feel like a reward, but going for a short, easy run that'll leave you feeling energised will. Downing eight glasses of water in one go will leave you feeling bloated, but one glass at regular intervals will leave you feeling refreshed.

I bet there's still one question you're dying to ask.

How long does it take until a behaviour becomes a habit?

Unfortunately, there are no clear-cut guidelines on this (everybody's different, after all). But there are estimates…

Here's how habit development usually occurs:

1. Initiation phase

This is when you'll select your desired habit, your trigger and the relevant context. In many ways, this is the most important phase. Unless you choose an appropriate trigger, place it into a relevant context and design your target behaviour in a way that you can keep it up (rather than making it so unpleasant that disadvantages outweigh advantages), you'll never manage to turn it into a successful habit.

2. Learning phase

Possibly the most cumbersome, the learning phase is all about practising your new behaviour in the correct context, and initiated by your chosen trigger. As it's all about endless repetition, some people simply lose interest. But here's the key: the more frequently you perform your new behaviour in the correct context, the stronger the strength of your eventual habit (also referred to as 'habit strength'). A period of several weeks is usually sufficient, and 10 weeks definitely should do it.

3. Stability phase

The stability phase has occurred when your behaviour happens automatically: you perceive your trigger, and you engage in your chosen behaviour. In fact, if you don't perform your behaviour, you'll feel odd, at a loss, as if you should be doing something… Hooray! You've developed a habit.

SIMILAR THEORIES – SAME THING

Incidentally, if you now think that all this talk about how to develop a habit sounds somewhat familiar…you'd be right!

In the previous section we discussed the value of establishing pre-performance routines to combat anxiety, develop focus, and get you in the right kind of mood to perform. But these kind of pre-performance routines are exactly like habits. As effective as they'll be once they're established (one small trigger will initiate the right kind of performance behaviour), they'll also need time to stabilise.

You might also have heard of the 'four stages of learning', a theory generally credited to the American psychologist Abraham Maslow[78]. It is generally associated to motor learning, but at its core it mirrors habit formation.

At the first stage called unconscious incompetence, people neither know how to perform certain skills nor realise their importance. I'm sure you'll agree that this is very similar to habit formation. You don't know a particular habit exists (or at least, you've never considered it for yourself), so you don't know what you're missing either.

The next stage, conscious incompetence, begins once an individual realises a particular skill is important, but are as yet unable to perform it. This stage is comparable to the habit initiation phase. Suddenly, you've realised how beneficial a particular behaviour might be. But while the motivation is there, the behaviour is a far cry from being a habit.

---

78   Maslow is better known for his 'Hierarchy of Needs Theory', which he developed in the 1940s. As his 'Stages of Learning Theory' does not appear in his major works, some people credit Noel Burch, employee at Gordon Training International with its inception in the 1970s.

The learning stage of habit formation can easily be compared to the conscious competence stage in motor learning – by now, individuals know what they have to do, but performing the behaviour takes conscious effort. However, as time goes by, the involvement of our rational part of the brain gradually decreases, until finally…

Unconscious competence, stability or automaticity is reached. A habit is formed, a behaviour has become second nature, the rational part of the brain has been superseded by the instinctive part.

So you see, regardless of whether we're talking habit formation, developing a psychological routine to induce the right state of mind or learning how to give the aid for a particular movement, mind and body have to run through the same stages every time.

There are no short cuts.

Every new behaviour, routine or skill takes time to develop and establish.

In conclusion, when you sit down to plan your season, take into account all the components that allow you to peak when you need to. Think of your own and your horse's fitness. Think of appropriate nutrition. Think of stable management, health care, psychological welfare. Think of how to turn yourself into the athlete you need to be. Think of developing the right mental skills. And give your horse and yourself plenty of time to get used to it all.

Really, it's the only way to become the best you want to be.

CHAPTER 13

THE WEEKS BEFORE: MOOD MATTERS

'I make sure that my horse is physically totally prepared and that I am mentally and physically ready.'

It's what Nick Burton did when he was still actively competing. It's what all the top riders do. Prepare themselves, and their horses. Physically. Mentally.

It's what you've done. At least, it's what you should have done.

You've set out your competitive season. You've got the 'Big One' to aim for at the end of your macrocycle, just like every other top competitor. And you've got medium-term stepping terms that'll mark the end of each mesocycle. That's when you're planning to peak. Just like they do.

Throughout your preparatory phase (the winter months), you've systematically trained your horse and yourself using your performance profile. You've even made a couple of new healthy habits, that you think might give you that extra edge.

And now you're at the start of the competitive phase, and you've got shows lined up as far as your – inner – eye can see.

Your first competition is next week. You know what your target performance is.

Using your training diary, you've really got to know your own and your horse's strong and weak points, meaning that, by now, you know precisely what you have to do once you're in the saddle. You've optimised his management regime and have developed a healthy lifestyle for yourself.

You've done everything you can to make sure that you and your horse are physically prepared.

What is more, you've worked hard on a task-orientated approach, and because you've been so structured and single-minded in your approach, you've gained confidence, have become more committed and have – finally – started believing in yourself. You've also practised your mental skills, so you know to focus on your performance and process goals, and leave the outcome goals to take care of themselves. You know precisely how much 'oomph' you need to ride at your best, and you've got a strategy in place to calm yourself down or hype yourself up. You know what you need to focus on and how to do it. You've got a focusing routine in place, supported by abdominal breathing, centring, a cue word. You've even come to grips with your dysfunctional thought patterns, even though you might still be somewhat unreasonable in your expectations (who isn't?!), so you're finally able to shut up that inner critic of yours. You've worked on your visualisation skills, and can use these to motivate yourself or to help you perfect a particular skill. You've even written (or drawn up) an imagery script.

You're pretty sure you're mentally ready, too.

Now all you need to do is hold it together. Emotionally, that is. Get yourself in the right frame of mind. And stay there.

If only it was that easy…

EMOTIONS MATTER…

For starters, what is the 'right frame of mind'? What does it feel like? Is yours different to that of other riders? And once you know, how do you get about getting – and sustaining – it?

If there's only one thing we know, it's this: when it comes to riding horses, being in the right frame of mind is an absolute must. Otherwise, we'll soon know about it.

Equine scientists still don't quite know how it works, but the fact is, horses are able to pick up on their riders' emotions. Research teams surrounding Dr Uta van Borstel from the University of Göttingen[79] and

---

79   Merkies, K., Sievers, A., Zakraisek, E., MacGregor, H., Bergeron, R., König von Borstel, U. (2014), 'Preliminary results suggest an influence of psychological and physiological stress in humans on horse heart rate and behaviour', *Journal of Veterinary Behaviour: Clinical Applications and Research*, 9(5), pp. 242–247

Professor Linda Keeling of the Swedish Agricultural University[80] have been able to show that when riders are anxious or nervous, their horses will respond with an increased heart rate. Dr Don Bridgeman from the University of Southern Queensland[81] demonstrated that compared to novice horse–rider combinations, heart rates in advanced dressage horse-rider pairs were synchronised.

Evidence that advanced riders are better able to keep their emotions in check? Quite possibly.

But even though we don't yet know how the – let's call it 'emotional exchange' – between horse and rider happens, we'd be safe to say that only riders who are at the top of their game emotionally are able to perform at their absolute best. Put simply, when you're down, stressed out, tired or feeling out of control in the run up to a competition, you aren't very likely to shine in the ring.

If you need any additional persuading, evidence in other sports has shown a direct link between different emotional states of athletes and their subsequent competitive performance. Sportsmen and sportswomen who felt depressed, demotivated, listless, angry or tired in the run up to a competition were generally unable to meet their own sporting standards. Feeling confident, full of energy and vigour on the other hand has been shown to provide the perfect backdrop to achieving personal bests.

Sounds simple enough?

So let's take a closer look at how the dynamics between emotion and performance work in real life.

We know a complex, intricate and powerful relationship between emotions, thoughts and behaviour exists. We know this because we've discussed the interaction throughout the chapters of this book. But even if we hadn't, you'd still know what I'm talking about because you are confronted with it every single day.

80 Keeling, L.J., Jonare, L. and Lanneborn, L. (2009), 'Investigating horse–human interactions: the effect of a nervous human', *The Veterinary Journal*, pp. 181 (1), 70–71

81 Bridgeman, D.J., Pretty, G.M., and Tribe, A. (2005), 'Exploring heart rate as an indicator of synchronization between dressage horse and rider at training and competition', paper presented at the 11th World Congress of Sport Psychology, Sydney, Australia

The things you do, the thoughts you think – they immediately impact on how you feel. Equally, the way you feel will influence the way you think and how you behave.

According to emeritus professor Nico Frijda from the University of Amsterdam[82], emotions are the sum total of a series of stages that involve a combination of thoughts, feelings, physiological changes, behaviours and, ultimately, emotions. They are an individual's reaction to an event that may be real or imagined and will result in a series of physiological, physical and behavioural changes.

Incidentally, understanding how an emotion develops can sometimes help to make sense of it too.

1. Cognitive appraisal

Events, situations, objects or persons can invoke all emotional reactions. This, initial, stage will always involve deciding whether, and how, a particular stimulus matters to us. Generally speaking, figuring out why and how an event, a situation, an object or a person matters can go a long way towards understanding the emotions that follow.

2. Context evaluation

Depending on your own background, your personal history, your goals, values and generally how you perceive the world, you'll come up with a way to deal with the event. This is all about your perceived coping resources. Do you possess what it takes to deal with whatever you're confronted with or do you think you're lacking some vital skills?

3. Action readiness

Depending on how you've ended up evaluating the context, your body literally readies itself for what lies ahead. If you think whatever you're facing

---

82   Frijda, N.H. (2007), *The Laws of Emotion*, Mahwah, Erlbaum

is easy, your muscles will soften and relax. If, however, you believe that the situation is going to be a real challenge or even a threat, your heart will beat faster, you'll feel your muscles tighten, ready to spring into action.

4. Expression

Your body's response will immediately translate into a physical expression. Your face might crease into a frown or break into a smile. Your arms might cross protectively in front of your body, or they might open in welcome. Emotions always go hand in hand with physical expression – that's why we are able to 'read' others around us, and are even able to gauge our horses' emotions. (Incidentally, that's also the reason why psychologists like to differentiate between feelings and emotions. Feelings are hidden, while emotions can be read in your bodies and on our faces.)

It should be obvious by now why moods and emotions have been found to be so incredibly important for performance in sport. What you feel will affect how you move. And how you move will affect your performance.

What is more, it's not just the emotions you experience on the day that will impact on how you'll do. Your emotional state weeks or days before you enter the ring can influence your readiness to respond (your 'action readiness'), your physical expression, and, as an immediate result, the way your horse reacts.

Here's the most interesting thing: the same emotion can affect people in different ways – and thus provoke a different competitive outcome. Imagine the following.

For weeks, you've been rushed off your feet, right until the day you're about to compete. Now you're feeling tired and listless. Your body feels like it's been filled with lead, and you can't even work up the energy to care anymore. On the morning of the show, you're so knackered, you simply can't motivate yourself to try anymore. But it's equally possible that all that fatigue dulls the usually oh-so-crippling feelings of nervousness. Instead of worrying what might or might not happen, all you can think of is getting through the day one step at a time – thereby managing, for the first time, to keep your focus on yourself and your horse.

Or how about this.

You've been treated unfairly at work, making you angry and annoyed. For days, you're pumped full of adrenaline, ready to snap at anybody or anything. Come competition day, you're so distracted, you're unable to focus on anything else other than what your boss said to you. The tension in your muscles interferes with any aid you give, and your horse gets increasingly more confused. On the other hand, perhaps you've decided to use the rage you feel to ride better than ever. You'll manage to channel all your energy into whatever it is you need to do to pull off a performance of a lifetime, just because you want to 'show them all'.

Here's another one.

The week before a competition you've met the love of your life, landed your dream job or were given the ultimate gift. For days, you've been so incredibly happy, you've been unable to eat, sleep, or even think straight. You've lost 10 pounds, simply because you've been on a constant high. As you enter the arena on competition day, it's as if you're floating. Your horse decides to join you and floats through his dressage test or over the course of jumps – or he might decide to throw in the towel because you're not paying any attention at all.

Three examples. Three types of emotions. Six different interpretations. The way we perceive the world around us, how we judge situations, how we react to them, and the effect such emotional reactions will ultimately have on our performance all vary according to the individual. That's also why psychology researchers define emotions as subjectively experienced reactions, rather than anything that is set in stone and can be measured objectively.

In essence then, how you interpret a situation will end up affecting you at the physiological, physical and behavioural level in all sorts of weird and wonderful ways – with a direct influence on how you ride your horse.

TIP OF THE ICEBERG

As you ready yourself for a competition, you'll obviously want to be able to achieve the kind of emotional or mood state that'll allow you to be at your absolute best.

It's what all the top athletes do. There's even a name for it. It's called the 'iceberg profile'. And here's why.

In the 1970s, a researcher and sport psychologist called William P. Morgan investigated emotional characteristics, 'mood states' of athletes in a variety of sports[83]. He soon noticed that successful individuals tended to score lower on negative mental states such as tension, depression, anger, fatigue and confusion. At the same time, these athletes scored higher on the positive mood state of vigour.

To illustrate his results, Morgan ended up drawing a graph in the shape of an iceberg. Vigour marked the tip, while the other, negative, mood states tapered off to either side.

Interestingly, athletes who didn't do all that well would generally demonstrate a mood profile much less pronounced, e.g. no vigour peak and no dropping off of negative mood states either.

His findings set the world of sport psychology alight.

Finally, the importance of psychological health (in the broadest sense) in sports had been demonstrated. Not surprisingly, Dr Morgan ended up emeritus professor at the University of Wisconsin-Madison and has been hailed as one of the most influential sport psychology researchers of his time. Still, his findings were slightly too good, or perhaps just a little too simple, to be true.

Not all successful athletes demonstrate a distinct iceberg profile, while not everyone who feels vigorous and not the slightest bit tense, confused, or depressed, is going to excel.

You'll know the reason, of course.

People, never mind whether they're marathon runners, cyclists or, indeed, riders, are all individuals. Some perform better when excited, others when calm and relaxed.

It's something we've already touched on in chapter 8, when discussing how much arousal you need. We called it your very own 'oomph'

83   Morgan, W. P. (1980), 'Test of champions: The iceberg profile', *Psychology Today*, pp. 14, 92-108

Morgan, W. P. (1985), 'Selected psychological factors limiting performance: a mental health model', in D. H. Clarke, & H. M. Eckert, *Limits of Human Performance* (pp. 70-80). Campaign, IL: Human Kinetics zone, as a synonym for the more common term of Individual Zone of Optimal Arousal.

INDIVIDUAL ZONES OF
OPTIMAL FUNCTIONING – AGAIN!

But while it is probably true that anxiety, nerves or arousal are often at the forefront of your mind when it comes to competing, other emotions can play an equally important role. Here, too, the teachings of Dr Yuri Hanin can help.

Remember him? He's the proponent of the Individual Zones of Optimal Functioning, which we discussed at length in relation to anxiety and arousal. As much as you'll need a certain intensity of arousal to perform at your best, you'll also require different levels of say, happiness, anger or fatigue. What's more, not all emotions that are generally considered negative have to end up undermining performance. Anger or annoyance (as long as it's not directed towards your horse) can spur you on to try a little harder. Tiredness might help you chill out a little. Equally, not all positive emotions are helpful. Happiness or joy can be distracting, gratefulness might not make you try very hard. The key is to figure out what helps you. Once you've done that, you need to try and invoke the right kind of emotions at the right time, and block or reshape the wrong emotions as and when they appear.

Even a top dressage rider such as Kyra Kyrklund appreciates that sometimes, even the best of us are in the grip of unhelpful emotions.

'Once in a while, everyone worries or is feeling anxious, that's perfectly normal.' [84]

Much more important is how you end up dealing, and reinterpreting the experience. Kyra calls it 'realistic optimism'. All it means is that sometimes there'll be moments where you don't feel at your best, but

84   Wolframm, I. (2012), *Dreamteam Pferd und Reiter: Persönlichkeitsbestimmung im Reitsport*, Stuttgart, Müller Rüschlikon

knowing what to do about it, how to cope is what separates the proverbial wheat from the chaff.

FINDING OUT WHAT WORKS FOR YOU

Don't know how to figure out which emotions in the build up to, and on a competition day itself, are helpful and which ones aren't?

If you've been keeping your training diary for some time, you'll want to use it now.

Identify a competition that went well. Your horse might have gone as you had hoped, you achieved your goals, you might have coped well with whatever the situation threw at you. Then, think of a competition that just didn't go according to plan. You felt harassed, your horse didn't listen, you simply didn't manage to get 'it' together.

Now think of the emotions or moods you felt at the time. (See over for a list to get you started, but there might be some other emotions you can think of. Just feel free to add them.) Rate their intensity on a scale of 0–10 (0 = couldn't feel it; 10 = incredibly intense). Next, think of whether the emotion or mood helped you perform (note down a '+' in the relevant column) or whether it was particularly unhelpful (identified with a '-'). Finally, note down your final score by simply joining up your intensity score with your plus or minus sign.

And there it is, the first draft of your emotional profile. In all likelihood, you'll find that there'll be positive emotions that were unhelpful, while some negative emotions were facilitative in some way. Just to reiterate, that's perfectly normal. The key is to recognise what is what.

So now that you know the kind of emotions that assist you in your equestrian endeavours, you'll need to determine which 'stimuli', e.g. events, situations, people, etc. evoke which kind of moods and emotions.

I've said it before, I'll say it again: life as a rider is very demanding.

You try and juggle training horses with a career either inside or outside the equestrian industry, a demanding family life and all those social obligations that tend to crop up at the most inopportune moments.

All too frequently 'a good night's sleep' becomes a definite thing of the past; the recommended five portions of fruit and vegetables per day

185

EMOTIONAL PROFILE				
	INTENSITY	HELPFUL (Good Competition)	UNHELPFUL (Poor Competition)	FINAL SCORE
UNWILLING				
TIRED				
UNCERTAIN				
BORED				
TENSE				
NERVOUS				
DISSATISFIED				
ANGRY				
EXCITED				
ENERGETIC				
MOTIVATED				
CONFIDENT				
EASYGOING				
SATISFIED				
OVERJOYED				
PLEASANT				

consist of fruit-flavoured wine gums (it says 'made from fruit extracts' on the bag so surely they count?); and being able to take even an hour of 'me-time' would be like winning the lottery.

But while missing the odd hour of sleep or eating a burger and fries once in a while isn't a big issue, taken together it all starts to amount to much more than the sum of its parts – and seriously undermines your emotional health in the run up to a show. By the time you get there, your body and mind will be running on (almost) empty and you'll have no emotional 'buffer' left to deal with the additional stress of having to compete. A minor inconvenience, such as a delay in the programme, or a small error in the test, all of a sudden becomes too much to handle – leading to a less-than-perfect performance! The managing of moods and emotions in the week(s) leading up to a show is therefore much more than a luxury – it can make or break a rider come competition day.

Luckily there are a number of ways to help you monitor how you feel from day to day.

1. Mind yourself

Mindfulness training, with the express focus on experiencing how you feel is one of the most popular trends today. Learning how to recognise and accept, without judgement or prejudice, current emotions can go a long way towards achieving your relevant peace of mind.

2. Go electronic

Simple apps for smart phones, that allow you to monitor how you feel from day to day are the modern alternative to keeping – or supplementing – your training diary already go a long way.

3. Visualise it

You might also wish to use your imagery skills to help you with monitoring your mood states. Simply visualise your optimal frame of mind as the proverbial 'half-full half-empty glass'. Anything you do that energises and motivates you will help fill the glass. Things that unduly tire you either physically or mentally, drain you of 'helpful' emotions and leave you with merely 'unhelpful' ones, will invariably empty the glass.

At the end of the day, it's all about finding the right balance. With yourself and your horses. Physically, mentally, emotionally. It's all about figuring out your weaknesses, working on your strengths and finding the right equilibrium.

But once you get the hang of this kind of 'mood awareness training' it'll ultimately result in you being able to deliver your personal best – every time.

CHAPTER 14

THE DAY BEFORE:
CALL ON YOUR CONFIDENCE

'Once the rider stops believing in his horse, it's all over! There won't be any more improvements in performance.'

Kyra Kyrklund[85]

Believing in your horse. Confidence in the partnership. Knowing that anything is possible. It's the foundation for any successful horse–rider partnership. It's why we do what we do.

That moment when the horse is listening to just a touch of your leg or the twitch of your finger. When all you need to do is think, and the horse is already responding. And yes, by now you know that sensation is called flow. But it still feels like magic.

Then it's the day before a show. Suddenly, you'll start to worry whether you've done everything you should have done. Just to be sure, you do one last training session. Put your horse through his paces one last time. But the harder you work, the harder it gets.

Now, the magic is gone. You start to panic. Will it ever return in time for tomorrow or has it gone for good? You feel completely rattled. Might you have forgotten how to ride? Your confidence has taken a serious knock. Time to recap and get yourself back on track…

THE IMPORTANCE OF SELF-CONFIDENCE

Here's something you've always known: confidence in yourself, in your ability to complete the job you've set out to do, is one of the most

85   Wolframm, I. (2012), *Dreamteam Pferd und Reiter: Persönlichkeitsbestimmung im Reitsport*, Stuttgart, Müller Rüschlikon

189

important moderators to competitive performance. It's a key aspect of mental toughness.

Throughout this book, you've worked hard on turning yourself into a mentally tough rider. You've developed the right kind of attitudes and necessary mental skills. You've honed your confidence. Confidence in your ability as a rider, confidence to be able to reach your goals, to control your nerves, to hold your focus, to think constructively, to visualise yourself performing well. Fitting all the mental puzzle pieces together so they end up forming one big picture – a mentally tough you.

You're ready. Able to cope, come what may.

Ideally, this feeling has become second nature, too. It's easy. Effortless. Natural. You have internalised self-belief, commitment, mental skills, the works, without even consciously having to think about it. You automatically assess your strong and weak points, you use appropriate coping skills, you're able to motivate yourself when things get tough.

Sounds good, doesn't it?

It's possible you haven't quite got there yet. Here's why.

Remember Professor Daniel Kahneman's ideas on how the brain works? Essentially, we are guided by two systems. System 1, our instinctive side, reacts unconsciously, is automatic, and, well, instinctive. System 2, the rational part of our brain, is slow, deliberate and meticulous.

At the beginning of habit formation, during the initiation and the start of the learning phase, the rational side of our brain rules the roost. Inevitably, that is what happens when you're still in the early days of developing solid mental toughness. Most of the time, this is not a problem. Your daily routine of going to the yard, getting on your horse and training is the framework that supports your newly found mental skills.

But sometimes, things change. Situations change. The day before (or the morning of) a competition the routine that's been supporting your fledgling mental toughness, is interrupted. You have to think about your next step, your next action. But because you have to think, you don't simply 'do' anymore. Suddenly, your mental skills don't feel all that solid.

That's when the first few niggles of self-doubt creep in: what if you can't do it after all? There's so much at stake (at least that's what you're telling yourself).

Suddenly, it's as if your mind's been wiped clear of everything you've worked on. So you start to panic...

The solution? Regain your self-confidence.

But first, let's take a quick look at how confidence develops in the first place...

DEVELOPING SELF-CONFIDENCE

According to one of the most cited psychologists of all times, Albert Bandura, Professor Emeritus of Stanford University, sport-specific confidence[86] is the ability to organise your existing skills in a way that enables you to meet the requirements of a (sport) specific situation. Really, it's all about balancing your skills with what the situation demands from you. And yes, your actual skills obviously play a role. It's much more important though that you *believe* you can manage – especially when it comes to developing confidence. This belief is developed, honed, maintained through four distinct sources.

1. Successful performance

This one's a no-brainer. If you managed to do something once or even several times before, you'll soon realise that, indeed, you have the necessary skills you need. The only problem arises when you're first starting out at something. Seeing that you've never done it before, how can you possibly know whether you've got the right kind of skills?

This is where both goal-setting and clever coaching come in. Mapping out, and then achieving, increasingly more difficult goals, will help you develop confidence as you grow more competent. Especially when you're still a bit of a novice being guided through the different steps by a good coach is invaluable. Still, even later on in your competitive career, coaching remains an important aspect of maintaining confidence. A coach telling you when you've done well (or what you might need to do in order to improve) is an important step to believing in yourself.

---

86 Throughout his work, Bandura refers to it as 'self-efficacy'. His key theories are captured in the following book: Bandura, Albert (1997), *Self-efficacy: The Exercise of Control*, New York, Freeman

2. Vicarious experience

In fact, having a role model, such as a coach or another rider you admire, is another potent source of confidence building. Observing someone else performing a skill (that's the vicarious bit) helps you to get a handle on how a skill is performed. That's why how-to films on Youtube are so popular. By watching others, you'll also realise that it is actually possible to do whatever you set out to do. Lastly, never underestimate the power of the competitive instinct in motivating you to learn a new skill. Something along the lines of 'If you can do this, so can I!'

3. Verbal persuasion

Think of how it makes you feel whenever your trainer or a fellow rider comments positively on your riding. Think of what it does to you when you receive above average scores in dressage, driving, vaulting or reining, in a style class in jumping or in a showing class. It's all feedback, telling you that you are good enough, that you are competent, that you know what you are doing. It gives you an enormous boost. Still, incessant praise is usually as unhelpful as continuous criticism. The former is unrealistic (nobody's perfect after all), the latter unrealistic (nobody does everything wrong either) and demotivating. To help shape confidence, feedback should either be positive when warranted, or constructive when necessary. So rather than merely picking on things, a good coach should acknowledge skills that are good and offer advice on how to improve those that aren't.

4. Feeling good

You'll know this like no other by now. Feeling alert and energised, rather than tense or hyper, focused on what matters most, yet not so tunnel-visioned that you miss relevant cues – all physical sensations that provide the background to optimal performance. And to building confidence. It's simple, really. If you feel strong enough to take on the world, you probably can.

It's not rocket science, is it? In fact, I bet you can recount many,

many examples of how your confidence has grown or been damaged by how you performed, how you felt, what someone else said to you or by what you observed others do.

When it comes to your 'riding-specific self-confidence' it will have been built over the years through a combination of what you've achieved, the role models you've had, what trainers, parents, peers or judges said to you and how you felt physically.

Incidentally, confidence in your horse's (or horses') performance is yet another dimension to your own confidence. Once again, it is founded on previous performances, comments other people made, and how he (they) feel when you're on board. Quite often, how you think of yourself as a rider, and what you think your horse can do are very closely interlinked. Which is why Kyra Kyrklund's message is important in more ways than one.

> *'Once the rider stops believing in his horse, it's all over! There won't be any more improvements in performance.'* [87]

Believing in your horse more often than not means believing in yourself, too.

So. Stop believing in your horse, and you won't improve. Stop believing in yourself, you won't either.

The problem is this: whenever you're facing a situation that's not entirely within your control and that, on top of everything, is also important to you (such as a competition), your immediate reaction will be to check if you've got all the skills you need. If you're not quite mentally tough enough yet, self-doubt will be rearing its ugly head. The worst case scenario (certainly from a sport psychological perspective) would be that you'll convince yourself that you're completely useless and might as well stay at home.

The reality of it is that you're simply failing to acknowledge the skills you have.

---

87   Wolframm, I. (2012), *Dreamteam Pferd und Reiter: Persönlichkeitsbestimmung im Reitsport*, Stuttgart, Müller Rüschlikon

All you need to do is shift your perception. That's what regaining confidence is all about. Shifting your perception from 'oh my, I'll never manage' to 'of course I can'. Realising that, really, you've got everything you need to deal with it. The best bit? You've already got all the skills you need to shift your perception. They are the mental skills you've spent all this time working on…

1. Successful performance - draw on your past

Remember what Charlotte said?

> 'I set myself three goals in dressage when I was 20. I wanted to ride on the team with Carl; I wanted to ride at Olympia Horse Show – I'd sat in the grandstands as a teenager thinking this is the best place in the world to ride; and I wanted to compete in the Olympics.'[88]

So that's what she did, ticking off her goals as she went along, with her confidence increasing along the way. Now remind yourself, if you will, of the goals you've set yourself. And no, it doesn't matter in the slightest that they don't involve either Olympia or the Olympics. The principle remains the same, regardless of the level you ride at.

It also doesn't matter if you've not yet achieved your long-term goal, nor any of your medium-term goals (you might only be at the start of your first mesocycle, after all). Still, you'll have achieved at least a number of short-term, process goals (otherwise you wouldn't be preparing for competition). There will have been quite a few training sessions that would have gone according to plan. You might even have competed at your first show of the season. Think of everything you've achieved, no matter how small, as another notch on the bedpost of your confidence.

But what if you've suddenly lost confidence in a specific skill. What

---

88   White, J. (14th May 2014), 'Charlotte Dujardin, the girl on the dancing horse, determined to stay No 1', *The Daily Telegraph*. html: http://www.telegraph.co.uk/sport/olympics/equestrianism/10831210/Charlotte-Dujardin-the-girl-on-the-dancing-horse-determined-to-stay-No-1.html

if you're not sure if you can ride that flying change, sliding stop or jump that fence? Well, just do as Mary King does.

> *'If I am hacking along, thinking about a big event in the next few days, I'll be imagining galloping round the cross country course and coming inside, and finishing in-time.'*

So go on! Visualise yourself performing well. Make sure you create an experience that's as life-like as possible and you'll fool your body and mind into thinking that you've already done it – boosting your confidence no end.

2. Vicarious experience – be inspired

Haven't got a real-life role model handy? No worries. All you need is a computer and internet access. Or a DVD player and a set of DVDs of the last international championships. Those will do, too. Sit down and watch your favourite horse–rider combinations strut their stuff, fly across country, whirl around on horseback, or perform impossible manoeuvres from up top of their driver's seat. Then, imagine yourself in their place. It doesn't matter if you're only about to compete in a novice competition. If they can do what they do, you can do what you do. It's all about the motivational power of watching others do what you love. Motivation, desire, inspiration – these are some of the most powerful driving forces to elicit top performance. It's what Tim Stockdale did when he was only a boy, sitting on top of a quirky, stubborn little pony.

> *'(…) I'd imagine myself at The Royal International with David Vine doing the commentary and introducing me to the millions of enthusiasts who were obviously watching me on TV. I'd canter Corky along the grass verge, humming the distinctive theme tune, imagining what it must be like to ride in front of a crowd cheering you on to victory.'* [89]

---

89 Stockdale, T. (2012), *There's No Such Word as Can't!* Croydon, Tim Stockdale

And if it worked for Tim Stockdale, it'll work for you, too!

3. Verbal persuasion – that voice in your ear

'Don't forget, some people want it to happen, some wish it would happen, go and make it happen.' [90]

Inspiring words, spoken by an inspiring trainer, leading to an inspiring performance. There can be little doubt that Carl Hester has been instrumental in helping Charlotte become the rider she is. That's because, as a trainer, he provided the feedback she needed to become ever more confident in herself.

If you've got a trainer who inspires you, you can always give them a call and ask them for a pep talk (I'm serious!). Perhaps you're lucky enough that they'll come with you to the competition. Discuss with them what you need to hear to boost your confidence (remember, your trainer might not even realise that you've lost faith. So don't be afraid to tell them.).

Still, there might come a time when you have to go it alone.

Never fear. Just think of what your trainer would say to you. Imagine the pitch and tone of their voice. Play it back in your head as a constant reminder that, yes, you are good enough.

Or you might prefer to come up with your own motivational slogan. Just like Viktor Brüsewitz did in times of extreme pressure. He simply thought

'Now we'll show them how it's done.'

effectively reminding himself that not only did he know how to vault, he knew (still does) how to vault like the best of them.

But if all else fails, and you realise that the negative voice inside your head just won't shut up, you need to go back and check your thought

---

90   Hester, C. (2014), *Making it Happen*, London, Orion Books. Carl's words are actually slightly adapted from Michael Jordan's original 'Some people want it to happen, some wish it would happen, and others make it happen'

patterns. Are you being a perfectionist? Do you think that you *must* win, otherwise there's no point in going? Do you think you *should* perform like this or that? Are you in danger of catastrophising perhaps? In short, are you being unrealistic in what you expect yourself to do?

Yes? Well, don't be!

On a serious note, though, try to reorganise your thoughts so that they become realistic and are in line with the goals you set yourself.

4. Feeling good – listen to your body

More often than not, if you've lost your confidence on the day before a show (or on the day itself), you fail to see your beating heart, the sickness in your tummy, the slightly sweaty hands, or the general unease you feel as anything other than stress. And stress, or so you've been taught for years, is bad.

Right?

Wrong (of course!).

Think back to how Nick Burton described symptoms of stress.

'I think if you wanted to describe anxiety that's part of the nerves that are part of the preparation. And that is something that I want to take place, otherwise it really doesn't matter anymore and I am not prepared because if you don't get a little bit of nerves, a little bit of jitters and a little bit of butterflies then you're not really preparing yourself to compete. If you're just riding, or running or walking, or whatever it is – you're not going to compete, and trying to do your best. So that's a very important part of it. And to deal with it is to actually use that as part of my focus (…).'

Once more, for emphasis. *Feeling slightly nervous is part of the preparation.* It's something you *want*. Something you *need*.

Now all you should try to do is to achieve the level of arousal that's appropriate *for you*, that'll allow you to be at your best. As it's the day before a show, you'll have a few options open to you. You might decide to go for a gentle run to get rid of the excess tension (don't overdo it, otherwise

197

you'll have to cope with muscle pain the next day). Or you might prefer to go for a sauna, or take a long, relaxing bath. You might go through your progressive relaxation routine, and do some breathing exercises to centre yourself.

Remember, the better you feel, the more confident you are. It's the best excuse to spoil yourself you'll ever get. Use it! And try to enjoy!

AVOIDING ROOKIE MISTAKES

You know what? You might be an excellent rider – but you're also human.

What I mean is this: in the heat (read: stress) of the moment, you might do things that, in retrospect, you can't quite believe you did. In your eyes, they fall under 'rookie' mistakes. Something only a beginner would do.

And yet, there you are, at the show, without your girth. Or bridle. Or saddle! You might have learned the wrong test. You forgot to check your start times, and now you're an hour late. You might have even got the date wrong (It's happened…)

Rookie mistakes, perhaps. Still, chances are, if they happen to you, they'll end up throwing you off guard. They might even push you over 'the edge'.

Don't risk it.

Be prepared.

Here's a list of the most common 'sport psych errors' you can make on the day before a show, or even on the day itself (but because you should do all of your preparation the day before, they are featured in this chapter).

1. To train or not to train?

Should you give your horse that one last workout the day before? It's difficult to give a definite answer, quite simply because it really depends on the kind of horse you've got, the discipline you're doing, and the level you're competing at. In essence, the core of the question is more about exercise physiology than anything else. The funny thing is that, most of the time, considerations about how a workout might affect the horse physically hardly come into it. More often, riders are inclined to try and fix that last little niggle, that one element they're unsure of. So they get on, and put their horses through their paces one last time.

Guess what? The problem, whatever the problem might be, hasn't gone away. It won't, either. At least not in this, last, training session. What is worse, because riders are often stressed, they anger more easily, get frustrated and become inconsistent. As a result, the horse might refuse to work altogether. A vicious circle, that's bound to spiral out of control.

Horses learn only through consistent, regular reinforcement *over time*. If they don't already know how to do it, one extra day won't crack it. What's worse, horses are likely to end up being tired and overworked the next day, i.e. the day of the show. Much better therefore to plan only a light training session, if at all, and only work on one or two easy movements, which you know you and your horse can do easily. It'll do wonders for your confidence!

2. To plait or not to plait (the day before)?

It might surprise you that I bring up the point of plaiting. It's such a small effort compared to all the other elements that are part and parcel of a competition. Still, plaiting requires the horse to stand still for, depending on your plaiting speed and your horse's mane, anything between 15 and 40 minutes. Standing still for that length of time requires the horse to be relaxed.

Remember those studies that show that horses pick up anxiety from their rider? The more nervous you are, either because of the show or because you really should be leaving in, oh, 20 minutes, the greater the likelihood that your horse will refuse to stand still. Trying to plait a horse that is jumping up and down and jiggling from side to side is not fun. Chances are, it'll stress you out even more. And yes, there's that vicious circle again! Stressed horse = stressed rider = stressed horse. So then, if you've got to set off relatively early the next day, and you know that your horse doesn't enjoy standing still at the best of times, consider plaiting the night before, when you still have lots of time. If you're really worried that your plaits are a mess the next morning, cover them with a pair of tights and wrap a rubber band

199

around each plait. All you'll need to do the next morning is remove the additional rubber bands, the tights, and, hey presto!, your plaits are still as pretty as how you left them – with the additional benefit that neither you nor your horse are unnecessarily wound up from the experience.

By the way if you're competing in a discipline that doesn't require plaiting – lucky you!

3. To party or not to party?

So do you go out the night before and let your hair down or do you stay in and cuddle up with a good book? Again, it's a tough one – unless of course, you've worked out what your optimal emotional state should be before a show. If you know, for example, that you perform best when you're happy and cheerful, bordering on hyper, and you know that a night out with your mates makes you very happy, staying at home alone would be a failsafe way to make you miserable. If however, you need quite a bit of time, peace and quiet to working up the right kind of focus, you might prefer to keep things low key. To get yourself in the mood – and to prevent yourself from overthinking and worrying about the next day's challenge – you might want to watch a video of the latest Olympics or read your favourite rider's autobiography (check the end of this book for a list of suggested titles). The key is to have a bit of an understanding of your own personality and what puts you in the right frame of mind. Most importantly, don't be swayed by what those around you are doing. Stick to your own plan!

4. Enough time

So you've planned the next morning like a military commander his next assault on enemy lines. Your alarm clock is set and, from that first ring, you've masterminded everything down to the last second. Excellent! Preparation is, after all, the first step towards success.

There's just one problem. It's called Sod's Law (if you're American, you'd call it Murphy's Law). Everything that can go wrong, will, in fact, go wrong.

This means that all your careful planning will come to nothing. And you'll end up extremely stressed. Much better, therefore, to give yourself a margin for error (in the event of your horse being covered in manure. Or your car not starting. Or roadworks on the way to the show).

If you like being early at a competition anyway, the extra half hour won't kill you. It'll just give you more time to look around, familiarise yourself with your surroundings, take your horse for a pick of grass before it's time to tack up.

If, however, you are the type that simply hates being early, because you can't bear to hang around and do nothing, come prepared.

Is there something your boss needed you to do in time for Monday? Take your laptop (and make sure you lock your car/lorry when you go off to compete!).

Never have enough time to read the latest gossip magazines? Here's your chance.

Addicted to computer games, but your kids always hog the iPad? Sneak it out of the house in the morning, when they're still asleep.

Having a distraction will prevent you from ruminating or from getting on your horse far too early and tiring him out. What's more, you won't get stressed because you're late! (By the way, it goes without saying that you should check and double-check your times before you even start working out how much time you'll need in the morning!)

5. Last minute panic

You get to the show, open the boot of your car, the cupboard of your trailer or lorry to get your tack – and your saddle pad is missing. Or your bridle. Or your whip. Anything, in fact, that is essential to your performance. Don't worry, it's happened to the best of them. But it needn't happen to you. Simply make sure you have a list of all the essentials taped to your grooming kit, or the inside of your trailer door. Write on it all the essentials you might possibly need, including spares. You might even decide to invest in a designated competition trunk, that holds everything from your horse's passport, his numnah, different types of studs and a selection of bits and a spare bridle. The night before, all you need to do is run through your list, item by item, and feel safe in the knowledge that there's no nasty surprise for you the next day.

It's what Nick Burton swore by to make sure he avoided getting into a flap the next day:

'I have my times, I have my kit in place, I have my hat where I know I can find it, I have a sequence of things around me, or a system around me that I know works.'

6. Well-meant advice

You've been experiencing some problems with your horse's contact. It's nothing major, but this evening, it's been at the forefront of your mind. As you're plaiting your horse, you're chatting away aimlessly to the lady who owns the horse next to yours. 'Oh yes.' she enthuses. 'I've had exactly the same problem. But the minute I tried this new bit, all my problems disappeared.' She sidles over to your stable and checks out your horse with a knowing smile on her face. 'Your chap is built in much the same way as mine. Why don't you try my bit tomorrow. I'll lend it to you.' Could her suggestion really be the end of your woes? It sounds almost too good to be true.

Yes. Of course it is. Too good to be true, that is.

Never, ever change anything on the day before a show. It's competitive suicide. You haven't trained in it, so you can't compete in it. It's that simple.

7. Bye-bye goals

You planned, you prepared, and then you planned some more. Your goals for this competition are the result of critical, yet constructive analysis of where you are right now, how far you've come and where you want to go. They make perfect sense and are your ticket to lasting, repeatable success. You know they are.

Then you read through the list of fellow competitors.

And all those carefully worked out goals are a thing of the past…

Because you simply must beat your arch-enemy. Or because, with a field like that, winning should be like a Sunday afternoon stroll in the park.

Or because you'll never score with that judge there.

I don't need to tell you of course that doubling back and, if you like, returning to the sport psychological dark ages will cause you nothing but misery.

Making your goals dependent on others, on external circumstances, will merely strengthen your conviction that you have no control over yourself and your own performance.

But think! If you convince yourself that you have no control, you'll have no confidence. No confidence, no performance.

So, as hard as it may be, even if you've got a sudden attack of the wobbles, stick to your plan. And if you're really struggling, here's another analogy that harks back from your days at school.

Cheat notes!

Actually – they really do work, at least in competition.

Once you have gone through the trouble of condensing your thoughts down so that they fit on a small piece of paper, they're as good as burnt onto the insides of your eyelids. You are unlikely to forget them in a hurry. All you need to do is think about a specific message to yourself, ranging from your riding-related goals (including the specifics, please!) to motivational pick-me-ups, commit them to a small piece of paper, and put them in the pocket of your riding jacket. Just like at school, chances are that whatever's on your 'cheat note' will stay with you for the rest of the show.

8. Lest you forget

Remember, this is supposed to be fun!

Just like all the other top riders, reminding himself that he truly loves horses and riding has been the key to success for German show jumping rider and trainer Dirk Ahlmann. In the show jumping world he is known for spotting and harnessing the enormous talent of horses such as the stallion Goldfever (successful under Ludger Beerbaum) and the mare Gitania (ridden by Marcus Ehning).

His advice for when things get tough, and you're in danger of losing the belief in yourself?

'Remember what's really important. Think of what the sport and the work with horses really means to you.' [91]

And that's really it, isn't it? It's what all of this is about. Knowing that this is what you're meant to do. It's what you've chosen to do. At the end of the day, it all comes down to your self-concept. Remind yourself of all those characteristics that make you who you are. A rider. First and foremost.

Now all you need to do is go to bed, safe in the knowledge that you're as prepared as you could possibly be for the day ahead.

---

91   Wolframm, I. (2012), *Dreamteam Pferd und Reiter: Persönlichkeitsbestimmung im Reitsport*, Stuttgart, Müller Rüschlikon

CHAPTER 15

ON THE DAY: PUTTING IT ALL TOGETHER

You trained for it, looked forward to it, perhaps you've even dreaded it (at least deep down). Now it is finally here – competition day! And that can only mean one thing: it's show time!

But let's face, even though you enter a show out of your own free will, it can be something of a double-edged sword: the potential for lots of fun and utter humiliation combined in one neat package! At least that's what that inner voice will keep telling you unless you teach it to do otherwise.

Really, this penultimate chapter is nothing more than a repeat performance. It'll remind you of all the things we've already discussed, the lessons you might have drawn from it all, and how to put everything in practice on the day. Just in case you don't think my word is good enough, I'll also remind you of some of the things the top riders of this world have said.

1.   Learn to love it

You know this by now and I really, truly hope that you've started to believe it too: a little flutter of nerves can be a very good thing. It makes you quicker in your reactions, helps you to focus on what matters most, prevents you from tiring easily and even makes you feel less pain. Rather than condemn it, welcome it. Appreciate that it's the sign your body needs to pull out all the stops. Remember Nick Burton:

> 'I'm competing, this is part of it, I feel nervous. I know that if I am feeling like that I am ready to compete, I am ready to do my best. If I go and I'm not interested, I'm not focused, I'm not nervous, I am not acting in a way that makes me perform well,

then I would be more concerned about not feeling anxiety than feeling anxiety. So I expect it and I want it. So that I know that I am ready.'

2.   Remind yourself that you can do it

One of the conditions of being able to turn anxiety into a feeling that's positive and helpful is to know you've got the relevant skills. How do you know? By having done it at home. This is what Adelinde Cornelissen says:

'Once I have everything under control at home, I want to find out if we can do the same thing somewhere else, in a different environment and under more difficult conditions.' [92]

That's exactly what you should be doing. And if you want to be absolutely sure you've got what it takes, make sure you train above the level you're planning to compete at. A competition is stressful enough without the additional worry of whether you and your horse are able to pull off all the movements in a test or cope with the height/technical requirements of a course. If you can be sure though that the demands of the competition are well within your capabilities, you'll be that much more relaxed before you start.

3.   Don't try and control the uncontrollable

Many people consider this the number one rule of mental skills training. All it means is that there is absolutely no point in worrying about the things that you can do nothing about on the day of the show. This includes, in no particular order, the weather, the judges or course designers, your fellow competitors, how nice their horses are, etc. (complete as necessary). It's been Kyra Kyrklund's recipe for years:

---

92   Wolframm, I. (2012), 'Mind over Matter: How mental training can raise your game', *Horse Sport International*, Issue 2

'I can't control how other riders present themselves at a show, which show they'll go to, or what scores the judges decide to give.'[93]

Focusing on elements outside of your control is wasted energy that you'd be better off spending on more important things, such as…

4. …controlling the controllables

It starts with seemingly mundane things such as having your times, your kit, the routine of how and when to tack up. Enough things can go wrong without your planning being one of them. So make sure you've got everything you need ready well before you leave. Also think of things that might go wrong when you get there, such as the zipper of your boot breaking or the weather changing just as you get there. While you can't plan for every eventuality, having a 'just in case' kit stored away in your car or trailer will give you additional peace of mind.

Then there's knowing yourself: do you prefer to arrive at the show ground with plenty of time to familiarise yourself with your surroundings, walk around a little, have a cup of coffee – or does waiting drive you crazy and you'd rather just get on and get started? Plan your day according to what keeps you in the best frame of mind. If you'd rather leave the yard with a few hours to spare, do that. If you hate to get there early, because it gives you time to worry, make sure you bring a book, a magazine, your iPad or anything else to help take your mind off things. Not everyone's the same, so don't just copy what your friends do.

But of course there's more. Make sure you know your optimal frame of mind, including how much 'oomph' you need, and how to either calm yourself down or rev yourself up. Be aware of the kind of thoughts that help you and those that don't. Visualise yourself doing well, and keep control of those mental images. Most importantly, know what you want to do, once you get in the saddle…

93   Wolframm, I. (2012), *Dreamteam Pferd und Reiter: Persönlichkeitsbestimmung im Reitsport*, Stuttgart, Müller Rüschlikon

5.   Set yourself goals

Remember, the best way to stay in control is to know exactly what it is that you want to achieve and how you are going to go about it. You want to ride a quiet test? Focus on keeping your joints (wrists, ankles, shoulders, etc.) supple and your muscles (upper arms, upper legs and so on) relaxed and 'off' the horse until you need to give an aid. You want to ride with more expression? Keep making sure your horse is 'on' the aids. Most importantly? Don't just focus on these goals in your warm-up, but keep reminding yourself of what you want to do while in the ring too.

6.   KISS - Keep it simple and specific

Of course your goals should be SMART. They should conform to the rules of goal setting as developed and approved by researchers throughout the world. But in the heat of the moment, you might not even remember, nor care, what SMART is. If that's the case, you can always try KISS – keep it simple and specific. Simplicity and specificity are key to knowing what you are supposed to be doing. So as you get on your horse, give yourself simple and specific instructions on how you intend to ride your test, the course, etc. You want your horse to be relaxed in the ring? Instruct yourself to loosen up through the shoulders and wrists. Your horse needs to move forward with more impulsion? Be adamant that your horse reacts to your leg the entire time while in the ring.

Incidentally, failing to keep things simple is one of the key issues Dirk Ahlmann has observed time and again. Quite often, he says, inexperienced riders (show jumpers) try and overcomplicate things.

> *'It could be so easy, though. A good rhythm and letting the fence come to you. That's enough.'* [94]

---

94   Wolframm, I. (2012), *Dreamteam Pferd und Reiter: Persönlichkeitsbestimmung im Reitsport*, Stuttgart, Müller Rüschlikon

7. Distract yourself

Do you worry yourself silly about all the things that might go wrong in the ring? Can you picture everyone laughing their heads off at your poor performance? Are you convinced the judges hate your horse? Rest assured, these thoughts are normal, most riders experience them at one time or another. But they're also unproductive and quite often end up undermining your performance. Rather than desperately trying not to think them though (which hardly ever works anyway), it's best to simply try and accept that you do (something along the lines of 'Hey, it's part of who I am, but I'm not going to let it affect me.') After that, move on and find something to do to take your mind off those negative thoughts. Playing a game on your smart phone, gossiping with a friend, and, while on board, focusing on what you are going to do (see commandment 12) and breathing correctly (see commandment 9) can work wonders.

8. Ignore others

I don't mean all the time, of course. But while you're tacking up, or already on your horse, you shouldn't be watching or paying attention to anyone else, be that fellow competitors, judges, spectators. You can't control them anyway – not what they're doing or thinking, not what they'll say to each other and not how they'll score your test. Incidentally, it's not always a good idea to watch other competitors beforehand either. If you only end up comparing yourself unfavourably, you should definitely leave it until after you've ridden.

Again, wise words from Kyra to support the message:

'I have learned not to compare myself to others but only to compete against myself.' [95]

---

95   Wolframm, I. (2012), *Dreamteam Pferd und Reiter: Persönlichkeitsbestimmung im Reitsport*, Stuttgart, Müller Rüschlikon

9. Breathe!

Ever asked yourself how come you can ride for an hour at home without breaking into a sweat, but a few minutes in the ring leave you completely knackered? It's because you forgot to breathe. Many riders will hold their breath for long periods in the ring, and, when they finally do take a breath, inhale into their chest cavity. The problem is, this type of – chest – breathing is very closely linked to the 'fight or flight response'. Breaths are short, shallow and jerky. Muscles are tight, tense and ready to jump into action – not ideal when you're doing a sport that, first and foremost, depends on fine motor control (i.e. small, very precise movements of your muscles). The answer? Remember to breathe into your belly, taking long, slow breaths. As you inhale, your belly should round a little, as if you're blowing up a balloon. Once you exhale, your belly will shrink again. Don't forget though that some practice is required, especially if you're not used to it. But in addition to relaxed muscles, you'll also end up with a calmer mind. Focusing on breathing correctly leaves little space in your head for any other worrying thoughts. (For more detailed instructions, read chapter 8).

10. Relax

Managed to control your breathing and need a bit more a challenge? All right, here goes. Work on relaxing your muscles on command. It's important to first start practising at home, though. Work your way through all the major muscle groups in your body, one after the other. First, tense them as hard as you can, then simply let go – and feel the tension drain from your muscles. Combine with a trigger word, such as relax or chill. Eventually, your trigger and relaxation will become inseparable. Once you get to the show, repeat your trigger word as and when needed to remove any superfluous tension that might (will) distort communication with your horse.

11. Listen

The power of music – don't underestimate it. The right tune can relax, stimulate, motivate, soothe, provide comfort or remind you of happy days.

So why not come up with a competition play list? You'll be able to magic yourself into the right state of mind at the mere touch of a button.

12. Focus

It's one of the key elements to performance. Being able to focus. Wayne Channon is adamant that no rider will get there without it.

> 'Everybody I know in the top of the sport, when they get on their horse, they are totally focused. They prepare themselves, and they work really hard at concentrating on what they are doing. This is crucial; you can't do it without that.' [96]

Attention, the right kind of focus, flow. When it happens, it's magical. Creating it is merely a question of practice. Remember, focus is a bit like the beam of a torch, highlighting merely those elements important to your performance, but leaving everything else in the dark. Especially if you're struggling to get into that focusing zone, you might want to make use of a trigger word or a pre-competition routine (see below), which your body will automatically associate with the right kind of focus.

13. Use a routine

Using a series of pre-determined positive (!) behaviours, actions or thoughts that your body and mind have learned to associate with another set of actions, moods or behaviours, will always, without fail, provide you with a sense of security. Routines can involve anything from the type of music you listen to on your way to the show, the way you tack up your horse or the way you structure your warm-up. Just before you enter the ring, you might also want to run through a set behaviour, words or phrases, such as a short gesture meaningful only to you, a deep breath, a trigger word, a visualised scene, and, finally, the command for your horse to get going. As long as the

---

96   Wolframm, I. (2012), 'Mind over Matter: How mental training can raise your game', *Horse Sport International*, Issue 2

routine is positive, helpful and enjoyable, you're good to go.

14. Be nice to yourself

Riders are possibly the most critical group of people I've ever come across. And that's a good thing too – when you're sitting on top of an animal with a mind of its own, you can't afford to be complacent. But if being critical about yourself is all you do at a show, you're missing the point… Too many riders keep telling themselves that they are 'rubbish', that they 'don't belong', that they 'might as well go home'. This kind of behaviour serves absolutely no purpose other than undermining your confidence (which is the last thing you need!). So try and be nice to yourself by complimenting yourself, for example on a well executed movement, your nicely turned out horse, or the planning you've done to prepare for this competition.

And if you cannot bring yourself to come up with a compliment, at least think of something constructive to say!

15. Visualise

You might have been doing it for years without realising that it's one of the most effective mental skills around: imagery. The ability to see yourself ride in your mind's eye. But now that you know it works, it might be time to make the most of it. Use it to improve on current levels of skill, by seeing yourself perform a tricky movement. Or motivate yourself by imagining yourself perform faultlessly at the top of your game. Or picture yourself calm and serene, in the right mental frame of mind. By visualising a desired outcome you're giving your mind and muscles a kind of 'blueprint' for the real action later on. Once again, though, remember that you should practise first to get as much control of your images as possible. Start out nice and easy, with images that are non-threatening and don't overly affect you emotionally. Involve all your senses too, so that you don't merely see yourself perform. You want to feel, hear, smell or even taste your mental experience. The results will speak for themselves.

16. Forgive yourself

So you've made a mistake. Big deal…

Seriously, even though it might feel like it at that particular moment, getting it wrong isn't the end of the world. If you're half way through your ride, give yourself positive instructions on what to do next. Mary King agrees:

> *'You have to try and not dwell on it, try and keep concentrating on what's ahead and not be thinking about a mistake you've just made.'*

Afterwards, remind yourself that this was just another competition (no matter how important it was), and that you'll simply work on it over the next few weeks. If this doesn't sound acceptable to you, check your assumptions. You might be trapped in a dysfunctional thought pattern. So rather than making unreasonable demands of yourself, try and learn from your mistakes. Lastly, think of the big picture. You're there, because you want to be.

17. Accept it

There'll always be days when things just refuse to come together. It's not your fault. In fact, it's nobody's fault. In the words of Mary King:

> *'Highs and lows are part of horse sports. Try and simply accept them.'* [97]

18. Enjoy it!

You've trained, you've prepared, you've spent lots of money and put in oodles of time. Most importantly though, at the heart of it all, it's about

---

97   Wolframm, I. (2012), *Dreamteam Pferd und Reiter: Persönlichkeitsbestimmung im Reitsport*, Stuttgart, Müller Rüschlikon

you and your horse. Adelinde Cornelissen thinks so too:

> 'Most importantly, I ride for myself. I ride because I enjoy it so much and because I love performing together with my equine partner.' [98]

Go ride. Have fun. Enjoy!

98   Wolframm, I. (2012), 'Mind over Matter: How mental training can raise your game', *Horse Sport International*, Issue 2

CHAPTER 16

THE DAY AFTER: AFTERTHOUGHT

So here we are then. The show is over. You've been there, you've done it, and you might even have got the t-shirt.

Hopefully, you'll have achieved what you set out to do and reached yet another milestone on your journey. Perhaps you've even reached your final destination. You're buzzing with the glow of dreams finally coming true, and you feel totally invincible. You're as good as shouting it from the rooftops: 'Bring it on, world!'

But there's still a chance that you didn't, that you hated the whole experience, that you didn't reach any of the goals you set yourself, and that you've sworn to yourself that you'll never, ever compete again. In fact, you're convinced that the whole world conspired against you. The organisers didn't help one bit, the judges had a continuous frown on their faces, the other competitors deliberately rode in your way or kept muttering under their breath intent on distracting you. The ground was too wet, too heavy, too soft or too uneven. The course was too difficult, too easy, too technical or just plain unfair. In a word, you hated it!

By now you know that it's only too easy to become emotionally wrapped up in something that means a lot to you – including competitions! You've invested a lot of time and money into doing what you love the most: training your horse(s). Being confronted with the hard reality of competitive results, especially when they are less than satisfactory, can result in the kind of emotional outburst that leaves those nearest and dearest to you diving for cover. Even when things worked out in your favour, everything came together beautifully and you are feeling so happy you could burst, the associated emotions, albeit positive, are of little practical use when it comes to figuring out what to do and how to do it next time.

Still, it's perfectly human to try and find reasons for why everything happens the way it does. In fact, an entire theory has been constructed just on this notion that people need to be able to understand, and even predict, why and how things happen in order to give their lives structure and stability.

FIGURING OUT THE REASON

The 20th century Austrian psychologist Fritz Heider developed a model of causal attributions that describes the cause for the outcome of an event as either internally driven, as a 'personal force', or externally determined, as an 'environmental force'. An individual's personal force includes aspects such as effort and ability, while external forces centre on task difficulty, other people and luck. As a dimension, this is called 'locus of causality', e.g. where does the cause for an event lie – anchored within a person, or somewhere externally? The interaction between internal ('I've got sufficient experience and skill at this show') and external forces ('The judge hates my horse' or 'The course is built fairly') generally causes a person to believe that they can – or cannot – succeed in any given task.

After much debate, revision and empirical testing, Heider's attributional model was reworked to include aspects of controllability and stability. The concept of controllability focuses on the extent to which an individual might be able to control either internal or external sources, while stability describes whether the cause of an outcome is stable and permanent, and thus cannot be changed, or unstable, malleable and therefore can be influenced.

How an individual perceives their own chance of changing the outcome of an event will be heavily determined by how they perceive the different dimensions of causality, controllability and stability. For example, if you think the cause for your success (or failure) is closely connected to your own levels of effort (causality of outcome is internal), and you're determined to simply try harder next time (level of controllability is high), you'll be convinced that you can change the outcome for the better next time (stability of the outcome is very small – it's likely to change). Nothing's set in stone as long as you try hard enough.

However, if you think that you're at the mercy of a judge (causality of outcome is external), and you think there's nothing you can do to convince him or her that your horse is good enough (level of controllability is low), you'll probably think that you'll never manage to change the outcome and, in the worst case, simply give up trying (stability of outcome is high – it's likely never to change).

You've probably already guessed it: having an internal locus of causality and thus believing yourself to be in control of events is preferable to thinking that you're a mere plaything of external elements.

Still, when people are disappointed or annoyed, there's a tendency to blame the environment for things going wrong. Rather than looking at what they themselves could have done differently, they're quick to point the finger at the judge, who didn't have a clue, the spectators who were distracting us, the photographer who used his flash far too often, or, worst of all, the horse…

It's a relief to be able to blame somebody – or something – else. To not have to take responsibility. To be able to say 'It wasn't my fault.'

If you're a guilty of blaming those around you, consider this: attributing your success to external, uncontrollable sources won't help you improve. It won't help you achieve your dreams. In fact, it'll make you feel helpless and undermine your self-confidence.

Much better to take a step back and look at things objectively.

First things first, though. Regardless of whether you're a winner or an 'also-run', it's important to realise that any competition holds an enormous amount of valuable information waiting to be unlocked.

So let's go through it one step at a time.

As you know, setting the right kind of goals prior to any competition is vital when trying to work towards long-term, sustainable success. In addition to providing a point of focus prior to a show, thinking about your goals can also be an excellent yardstick once you're packed up and ready to go home – and determine where the locus of causality really lies.

Whether you did well or not – or if you're still in a state of utter confusion as to what actually happened – you need to ask yourself this question: did you really work towards achieving the goals you had previously set – or did you perhaps readjust them at the very last minute?

Maybe the warm-up had gone so well that you changed your goals just as you were about to enter the ring. You decided that you could afford to raise the bar that little bit higher, aiming for a higher score or a faster time. Or perhaps you got so intimidated by your fellow competitors that you decided you'd be happy to merely 'get round', and subsequently stopped riding to your full potential.

But when you didn't achieve those new, revised, goals, your immediate instinct was to blame the judges, the competitors, the venue, your horse, any external source you can think of, when, in fact, it was you who altered the conditions of your performance…

Changing your goals at the last minute can mean pulling the proverbial rug out from under your and your horse's feet. At home, all your training was geared towards one goal, and on the day itself you changed it…

There can't be any doubt who's responsible, can there?

Once again, placing the blame on an external source can feel cathartic in the heat of the moment, but it'll leave you feeling frustrated and incompetent in the long run.

But even if you ended up performing at your absolute best, you should still take a good hard look at why this was: did you manage to pull off what you set out to do?

If so, well done! All praise to you, and you should, quite rightly, attribute success to yourself.

On the other hand, is it possible that you were – dare I say it – lucky? It is possible that, for once, circumstances were working in your favour and that you ended up with a better score than you really deserved?

Yes?

It's okay to be really pleased, of course.

As we've discussed time and again, Lady Fortuna of equestrian sports is fickle at best. In all likelihood, there'll be plenty of times, when things won't go in your favour so luck and bad luck will even out in the long run.

So why am I raising this?

While it is undoubtedly highly dangerous to attribute failure to external sources, it is equally unproductive to keep taking credit for something that's not really yours. And that goes for sport too.

Knowing what you did and why you did it remains at the forefront to maintaining control – of yourself, your horse and your performance.

So, what should you do? Well, once the first emotional response has subsided, back up a step and figure out what it is that you wanted to do versus what you actually did.

Did your preparation in the week(s) leading up to the show go as planned? Did you arrive at the show in an optimal frame of mind? Did you warm up your horse the way you know works best? Did you ride your course, your test, your show just the way you had planned? If you didn't, was there a (good) reason for it? Perhaps circumstances changed at the last minute, meaning you had to change course, change tack, change goals.

As long as you know what you were doing and why you were doing it, all is well.

Then, and only then, will you stay in control. Only then will you be able to take relevant measures such as adjusting your training schedule, your goals, your thought patterns or emotional state of mind accordingly.

Most importantly though, when you feel that you're in control, sitting in the saddle and – literally and figuratively – holding the reins, will you be able to achieve whatever it is you set out to achieve.

It's what mental toughness is all about.
It's about knowing who you truly are.
About being able to cope when things get tough.
It's about motivating yourself, day after day.
About staying committed, no matter what.
It's about building a network that'll support you.
About putting a stop to self-sabotage.
It's about setting goals.
About managing stress so it'll help rather than hinder you.
It's about focus, flow and being in the zone.
About seeing yourself succeed.
It's about preparation, and planning.
About knowing yourself and your horse.
It's about wanting the best for both of you.
About enjoying yourself.
It's about developing the perfect mind. For a perfect ride.

SUGGESTED READING

A. P. McCoy (2011), *My Autobiography,* London, Orion Books

Carl Hester (2014), *Making it Happen,* London, Orion Books

Claire Lomas (2014), *Finding my Feet*, Melton Mowbray, Claire Lomas Books

David Broome (1971), *Jump-off*, London, Stanley Paul

Hans Günter Winkler (1966), *Halla, meine Pferde und ich,* Hannover, Fackelträger-Verlag

Ian Stark, Jenny Stark and Kate Green, *Stark Reality,* David & Charles

Inga Wolframm (2012), *Dreamteam Pferd und Reiter: Persönlichkeitsbestimmung im Reitsport*, Stuttgart, Müller Rüschlikon

Joyce Heuitink and Harry Schoorl, (2010), *Het Loboek voor de dressuur ruiter,* EiS Expertise in Sport

Katrin Kaiser (2008), *Meredith Michaels-Beerbaum: Pferde sind mein Leben,* Köln, Schneider Buch

Kyra Kyrklund and Jytte Lemkow (2009), *Dressage with Kyra: The Kyra Kyrklund Training Method*, Wykey, Kenilworth Press

Mark Todd (1998), *So Far, So Good*, London, Weidenfeld & Nicolson

Mark Todd and Kate Green (2012), *Second Chance: The Autobiography*, London, Orion Books

Mary King (2009), *The Autobiography,* London, Orion Books

Nick Skelton (2001), *Only Falls and Horses,* Greenwater Publishing

Pippa Funnell (2005), *The Autobiography,* London, Orion Books

Richard Dunwoody (2000), *Obsessed*, Headline Book Publishing

Richard Dunwoody and Clement Wilson (2009), *Method in my Madness, 10 Years out of the Saddle*, Chatham, Thomas Brightman

Susanne Strübel (1999), *Erfolg ist kein Zufall,* Stuttgart, Kosmos

Tim Stockdale (2012), *There's No Such Word as Can't,* Tim Stockdale Publishing

William Fox-Pitt and Minty Clinch (2007), *What Will Be,* London, Orion Books

Brian Hoey (2007), *Zara Phillips*, Published by Virgin Books (2007), Reprinted by permission of The Random House Group

INDEX
OF NAMES

Todd, Sir Mark   17, 43, 57
Tomlinson (née Bechtolsheimer),
    Laura 160

van Grunsven, Anky 16, 17, 28,
    134, 167

Wathelet, Gregory 112, 113, 114,
    119
Werth, Isabell 16, 28, 134
Whitaker, John 16, 17